AMERICAN VOICES:
Movers and Shakers

A Low Intermediate Reading Text

Julia Jolly

Dominie Press, Inc.

Publisher: *Raymond Yuen*
Executive Editor: *Carlos A. Byfield*
Editorial Assistant: *Bob Rowland*
Designer: *Gary Hamada*
Cover Designer: *Carol Anne Craft*

Published by:

Dominie Press, Inc.
1949 Kellogg Avenue
Carlsbad, California 92008 USA

ISBN 0-7685-0007-9
Printed in Singapore by PH Productions Pte Ltd

1 2 3 4 5 6 IP 00 99 98

TABLE OF CONTENTS

ACKNOWLEDGMENTS

I wish to thank all of the people who supported the writing of this book. If I have inadvertently forgotten anyone, please chalk it up to middle-aged memory, rather than intent.

Many thanks to my editor, *Carlos Byfield*, who has shepherded several of my textbooks into publication and who first approached me with this project. Thank you for your vision, patience, and stubborn persistence.

Ongoing thanks to the community in which I teach. My fellow instructors, administrators, technical experts, and students at Sacramento City College have made this project possible:

Kirk Wiecking, Dean of Learning Resources, for unfailing encouragement and courtesy; *Terry Hajek*, Media Resources, who got the audio project off the ground, helped with the scheduling nightmare of producing the audiotape, and never failed to come up with solutions to problems; *Bob Bickley*, who was gracious and helpful with the "American voices," who never lost heart or patience, and whose technical expertise made possible the last leg of this project.

Marie Larson, whose idea it was to include Frank Fat, a local Sacramento hero, as one of the focus personalities and whose techniques for teaching and analyzing reading inspired some of the activities in this text.

Assorted Campus personalities, who freely contributed their expertise: *Nancy Olender*, Computer Services, who copied the disks from my antediluvian computer onto hard disks for "real" computers; *Sandy Warmington*, Library Services, who came up with information on Frank Fat at a moment's notice; *Walt Sherwood*, Dean of Language & Literature, and *Dr. Larry Hendrick*, Dean of Instructional Services, who brainstormed over lunch a list of campus personalities who could do the "American voices" for the audiotape.

The "American Voices," featured in the audiotape are the voices of instructors and counselors at Sacramento City College. We tried to duplicate, to the degree possible, the ethnicities and geographic backgrounds of the focus personalities in the text in the accompanying voices of the audiotape. I am very grateful to:

Dr. Cecilia Moralez-Hart, the voice of Guadalupe Quintanilla
Dr. Susan Schiller-Chainey, the voice of Ruth Bader-Ginsburg
Juan LaChica, the voice of Cesar Chavez
Robert Jordan, the voice of Colin Powell
Karen Kunimura, the voice of Patsy Takemoto-Mink
Jonathan Brosin, the voice of Steven Spielberg
Adrienne King, the voice of Shirley Chisholm
Richard Yang, the voice of Frank Fat
Beora Hart, the voice of Bill Cosby
Terry Hajek, the introductory voice and "Structure Analysis" voice

Thanks to the 3W students, who "tested" the various reading activities in the text. Their responses to the material helped to shape its final form.

And, finally, I want to thank *Lynn Savage* and the ESL Institute, in which I was a teacher trainer for over seven years during the 1980s. In "training" teachers of reading, I was also trained and learned what to look for in a reading text.

GUADALUPE QUINTANILLA

"Success is a journey. We're all in the journey."

PREREADING

What challenges have you faced in your particular journey?
Circle the challenges below that apply to you.

Health   **Physical Disabilities**   **Language**   **Making Friends**

Look at the picture above. Do you think that this woman has faced challenges like the ones you have faced?

List the three biggest challenges in your life, in order of importance.

1. _____

2. _____

3. _____

GUADALUPE QUINTANILLA: A SUCCESSFUL JOURNE

1 The year was 1985. The place was New York City. At this meeting of the United Nations, the alternate ambassador from the United States was speaking. She had long, black, curly hair and expressive hands. She talked about communication between different groups of people and the need to understand each other. Dr. Guadalupe Quintanilla addressed her audience in both English and Spanish. As she spoke, she remembered her own struggles with the language of her adopted country.

2 Guadalupe entered the first grade in the United States at the age of thirteen. Seven years older than most of the students in her class, she was also isolated by her limited English. In her native Mexico, she had been an excellent student, even helping other children to learn to read in Spanish. However, at this school, she was given an IQ test in English. She was labeled "mentally retarded" because of her test results.

3 Miserable in this class, she kept to herself. Because there was no second language instruction and no Spanish used in school, she had no way of communicating. Guadalupe decided that she could not learn; she became a dropout at thirteen.

4 She did not return to school until ten years later, when she began to help out in her own children's elementary school. By this time, she was a contented wife and mother. But she was worried about her children. They were not doing well in school. She wanted to help them with their work, but once again, English was an obstacle. This time, Lupe decided that she was going to learn English. She was not going to wait until her own boys dropped out of school. She would conquer English!

5 Lupe's path, however, was not easy. She tried to enroll in programs at a hospital, a high school, and a community college. Everywhere she went, the door was closed. Her school records labeled her a "non-learner." She didn't have a high school diploma. No one wanted to take a chance on Guadalupe Quintanilla.

6   Finally, this determined young woman convinced the registrar at Texas Southmost College to give her a chance. He obtained a special permit to enroll her in English classes. This was all Guadalupe needed: one open door! Despite long hours commuting to school on the bus, juggling her home duties with her homework, and waking up before dawn to find a few precious hours to study, she was successful. She made the Dean's List her first semester.

7   From then on, there was no stopping Guadalupe Quintanilla! She went on to earn a bachelor's degree in biology, graduating with honors from Pan American University. A master of arts in Spanish and Latin American literature soon followed, and just five years later, in 1976, she earned her doctorate in education. Guadalupe's life was a whirlwind of activity school, jobs, and home life. But for her, the biggest achievement was the success of her children. They were no longer struggling in school. With their mother's help at home, along with her example, they began to excel. Following in their mother's footsteps, they went on to college and chose careers in law and medicine.

8   Guadalupe Quintanilla had proven herself. She had also helped her sons and daughter find paths to success. But did she stop there? She didn't even slow down! Lupe discovered the importance of communication skills, and she began to reach out to her community. In 1977, she helped to establish the Cross Cultural Communication Program in Houston, Texas, which improved relations between the

police force and the Spanish-speaking community. This program was so successful that it has been duplicated all over the country. Because of Guadalupe's work in education, former President George Bush asked her to be on a national commission dealing with the educational needs of Hispanic students.

 9   Guadalupe Quintanilla has become an expert on communication. The frightened thirteen-year-old girl who dropped out of school has become an advocate for children in education. Guadalupe practices what she preaches: *Querer es poder*–Where there is a will, there is a way.

LISTEN AND SCAN
Listen to the questions on the tape. Stop the tape after each question. Scan for information, and write your answers on the lines below.

1. What made Guadalupe different from the other children in her first grade class?

2. Who gave her a chance to return to school?

3. What careers did her children choose?

4. What kind of program did Guadalupe set up in Houston, Texas?

Paragraph	Line	Response
1. _____	____	_____
		_____
2. _____	____	_____
		_____
3. _____	____	_____
		_____
4. _____	____	_____
		_____

PUTTING THINGS IN ORDER

The sentences below are **paraphrases**. A paraphrase is a sentence with the same meaning as another sentence, but using different words.

Work with your partner to find the sentences in the reading with the same meaning. Underline those sentences.

Then, number the paraphrases from 1 to 10, in the order in which they occur in the reading.

_____ Guadalupe's children were not succeeding in their classes.

_____ Dr. Quintanilla spoke to the gathering in two languages.

_____ Because of her score on the IQ test, the teachers thought that Guadalupe could not learn.

_____ Lupe knew that communication was important, and she started to share this knowledge with her community.

_____ Guadalupe left school in her early adolescence.

_____ The registrar sought special permission, allowing Guadalupe to attend English classes.

_____ Guadalupe could not find anyone who would give her a chance.

_____ Her sons and daughter followed her example and chose professional careers.

_____ Guadalupe graduated with honors and received a bachelor's degree in biology.

_____ Lupe made a decision to master the English language.

Where did you find the sentence?

Beginning with Sentence 1, identify the paragraph and line.

Sentence	Paragraph	Line	Sentence	Paragraph	Line
_____	_____	_____	_____	_____	_____
_____	_____	_____	_____	_____	_____
_____	_____	_____	_____	_____	_____
_____	_____	_____	_____	_____	_____
_____	_____	_____	_____	_____	_____

CHARACTER ANALYSIS: SUPPORT YOUR POINT OF VIEW

List three adjectives that describe Guadalupe Quintanilla.

1. _____

2. _____

3. _____

Share your adjectives with the members of your group.

Now work as a group to analyze the following:

What did Quintanilla do?	Paragraph	What does this tell us about her?

_____

_____

_____

_____

_____

_____

What did Quintanilla say?

_____

_____

What did other people say about her?

_____

_____

Look at your adjectives at the top of the page. Can you support them with sentences from the reading? What paragraph? What line?

	Adjective	Paragraph	Line
1.	_____	_____	_____
2.	_____	_____	_____
3.	_____	_____	_____

INTERPRETATION

False Statements

The following statements about the reading are **incorrect. Find** the words that make the statements incorrect and cross them out. **Replace** the incorrect words with the appropriate words from the reading.

Share your responses with the members of your group. Then, **identify** the paragraph where you found the information. **Write** the number of the paragraph on the line before each statement.

___ 1. In the first grade, Guadalupe was isolated by her limited Spanish.

___ 2. Lupe made the Dean's List during her second semester in college.

___ 3. Guadalupe became an expert on language acquisition.

___ 4. In 1995 Guadalupe Quintanilla spoke to the United Nations.

___ 5. Lupe decided to return to school to help her husband.

___ 6. After she earned her doctorate in education, Quintanilla's life was calm and quiet.

___ 7. Quintanilla's sons and daughter chose careers in business and law.

___ 8. The Cross Cultural Communication Program in Houston, Texas improved relations between English speakers and Spanish speakers in the community.

CAUSES AND EFFECTS

Below are a list of causes and a list of effects from the reading. Match the two.

a. Guadalupe couldn't speak or read English.

b. Quintanilla set up a cross cultural communication program.

c. Guadalupe decided that she couldn't learn.

d. She was worried about her children.

e. She woke up before dawn.

___ She decided to conquer English.

___ She made the Dean's List at Texas Southmost College.

___ Her IQ test results were low.

___ Community relations improved.

___ She dropped out of school.

Listen and Scan

Listen to these paragraphs from the reading. **Scan** the paragraphs while you listen. Then, **identify** the main idea, paragraph number, and line.

Main Idea

_____

_____

Paragraph _____   Line ___

Main Idea

_____

_____

Paragraph _____   Line ___

Main Idea

_____

_____

Paragraph _____   Line ___

Notice the position of the main ideas in these paragraphs. Is the main idea always in the same place in each paragraph?

Now that you have identified the main ideas, **find** the details that support them. **Write** the paragraph numbers in the column on the left. Then **list** the details that support the main idea in each paragraph.

Paragraph   **Supporting Details**

_____   _____

Paragraph   **Supporting Details**

_____   _____

Paragraph   **Supporting Details**

_____   _____

WORD WATCH

Some of the vocabulary in the reading may be new to you. In the groups of words below, **circle** the **one** word that does not fit in the group. Then, **share** your results with your group.

In and Out

1. isolated   miserable   elementary

2. determined   frightened   precious

3. practices   expert   advocate

4. addressed   spoke   remembered

5. doctorate   homework   masters

6. struggling   achievement   success

With your class or in groups, **identify the part of speech** of each group of words and **discuss** why each word you chose does **not** fit.

OPPOSITES

In the numbered paragraphs, **find** the words that are the **opposite** of the words listed below. Then, **write** the opposite words on the blank lines.

1. Paragraph 3   contented   _____

2. Paragraph 6   poor   _____

3. Paragraph 1   native   _____

4. Paragraph 4   fail   _____

5. Paragraph 9   brave   _____

6. Paragraph 7   open   _____

7. Paragraph 1   forgot   _____

8. Paragraph 4   discontented   _____

Positives and Negatives

Make a list of words from the reading that describe Gaudalupe Quintanilla.**Identify** the words as positive **(+)** or negative **(–) by circling the appropriate symbol.**

_____   +   -   _____   +   -

_____   +   -   _____   +   -

Guadalupe Quintanilla has had some challenges in the journey of her life. She learned to meet some of those challenges.

List below some of the obstacles that Quintanilla had to overcome.

What are some of the obstacles in your life? **List** a few of the obstacles.

Now **number** the obstacles in both lists, from the most difficult (1) to the least difficult (4).

	In Guadalupe's Life		**In My Life**
___	_____	___	_____
___	_____	___	_____
___	_____	___	_____
___	_____	___	_____

Discussion Questions/Reading Journal Topics

1. In what ways does Guadalupe Quintanilla remind you of people in your family or community?

2. What do you have in common with Dr. Quintanilla?

3. Is there anything you would like to know about Guadalupe Quintanilla? Explain.

4. Why do you think this woman was so successful?

RUTH BADER GINSBURG

"Ruthless Ruthie": First in her Class

PREREADING

The nickname "Ruthless Ruthie" was given to Ruth Bader Ginsburg at Columbia University, where she was a law student.

What do you think her classmates meant by the word **ruthless**?
Circle one of the possible synonyms below.

Without a Name   Without a Female Friend
Without Giving Up   Without Hope

Look at the picture above. What adjectives might describe this woman?

List your adjectives below.

1. _____

2. _____

3. _____

RUTHLESS RUTHIE: FIRST IN HER CLASS

1   When Ruth Bader Ginsburg was a student at Columbia Law School, her classmates called her "Ruthless Ruthie" because of her determined attitude about her schoolwork. She believed in giving 100 percent in everything she did. She wasn't always successful, but she didn't give up.

2   Ruth was lucky. Even though she grew up during a time when opportunities for women were limited, her parents encouraged her to be ambitious. Her mother, especially, believed in equal opportunities for women and urged her daughter to use her talents. Ruth lost her biggest supporter when her mother died the day before her high school graduation, but she never forgot her mother's strong belief in women's rights.

3   In Ginsburg's first year of college at Cornell University, she met the person who would be the strongest supporter in her future career. Both Martin Ginsburg and Ruth planned to be lawyers. After their marriage in 1954, Martin enrolled in Harvard Law School. Ruth wanted to attend the same law school, but at this time, it was an all-male school. If she applied, would she be accepted? What about their new baby, Jane Carol? Could Ruth attend school and take care of Jane at the same time? Even Ruth's own father thought she should forget about law school and become a teacher. However, with the strong support of Martin, Ruth made the decision: she would study law.

4   Ruth was in the right place at the right time. In 1956, the year she applied, Harvard Law School decided to admit women for the first time. There were nine female students in a class of 400. (Today, law schools have both male and female students in almost equal numbers.)

5   At Harvard, Ruth excelled, just as she had at Cornell, in spite of discouragement from some professors. Ruth went on to graduate from Columbia Law School, where she tied with another student for "first" in her class of 1959. It was at Columbia that Ginsburg earned the name "Ruthless Ruthie." She was serious about her studies.

6   Despite her success in school, Ruth faced many obstacles when she entered the professional world. While male classmates found jobs as law clerks, Ruth worked as a legal secretary because it was the only position she could find. Ruth had three strikes against her in 1959: she was a woman, she was the mother of a child, and she was Jewish. No one wanted to hire her.

7   It took Ginsburg four years to get a job which suited her abilities. During these four long years, she learned about sex discrimination, racial discrimination, and the frustration of facing closed doors; but Ruth didn't give up. Finally in 1963, she got a job as an assistant professor at Rutger's School of Law in New Jersey. "Ruthless Ruthie" became one of the first women in the country to have a job as a professor of law. Another big first!

8   During her years as law professor, Ruth Ginsburg worked tirelessly for equal rights for women. Her own experience with discrimination inspired a lifelong battle for "equality under the law" for both men and women. For example, in 1973, she took a case involving the U.S. military. At that time, the wives of men in the military received more benefits than the husbands of women in the military. Arguing that this practice was unfair to husbands, Ginsburg took the case to the Supreme

Court and won. In the 1970s she went before the Supreme Court with six different cases on sex discrimination, winning five out of six.

 Given Ginsburg's record of achievement and commitment to equality, her appointment as a justice on the Supreme Court is not surprising. When President Clinton appointed her in 1993, he stated that he was looking for someone with a "big heart." He found Ruth Bader Ginsburg, who became the second woman in history to sit on the U.S. Supreme Court: another big "first" for "Ruthless Ruthie," and a big plus for the United States.

LISTEN AND SCAN

Listen to the questions on the tape. Stop the tape after each question. Scan for information, and write your answers on the lines below.

1. After law school, why did Ruth have difficulty finding a job?

2. What happened in 1963?

3. Why did her classmates call her "Ruthless Ruthie"?

4. Who was Ruth's biggest supporter after her mother died?

Paragraph	Line	Response
1. _____	____	_____
2. _____	____	_____
3. _____	____	_____
4. _____	____	_____

The sentences below describe events in Ruth Bader Ginsburg's life.

Work with your partner to find the events in the reading.

Underline those sentences.

Then number the paraphrases below from 1 to 10, in chronological order.

____ Ruth was one of the first women in the U.S. to become a law professor.

____ At Columbia, Ginsburg was at the top of her graduating class.

____ Jane Carol Ginsburg was born.

____ Law schools admit almost equal numbers of men and women.

____ Ginsburg won five Supreme Court cases related to sex discrimination.

____ Ginsburg's father thought she should become a teacher.

____ Ginsburg worked as a legal secretary.

____ Harvard Law School decided to admit female students for the first time.

____ Ruth Bader Ginsburg became the second woman in history to sit on the U.S. Supreme Court.

____ Ruth's mother died.

Where did you find the sentence?
Beginning with Sentence 1, identify the paragraph and line.

Sentence	Paragraph	Line	Sentence	Paragraph	Line

List three adjectives that describe Ruth Bader Ginsburg.

1. _____

2. _____

3. _____

Share your adjectives with the members of your group.
Now work as a group to analyze the following:

What did Ginsburg do?	Paragraph	What does this tell us about her?

What events changed Ginsburg's life?

_____

_____

Look at your adjectives at the top of the page.

Can you support your adjectives with sentences from the reading? What paragraph? What line?

	Adjective	Paragraph	Line
1.	_____	____	____
2.	_____	____	____
3.	_____	____	____

INTERPRETATION

Fact or Opinion?

Some of the following statements about the reading are **facts** and some are **opinions**. Identify which are **facts (F)** and which are **opinions (O)**. Underline the words in the **opinion** sentences that identify an opinion.

_____ 1. Ruth's Columbia classmates called her "Ruthless Ruthie."

_____ 2. Justice Ruth Bader Ginsburg is the most intelligent member of the U.S. Supreme Court.

_____ 3. Ruth's husband encouraged her to succeed.

_____ 4. Ginsburg's parents didn't attend college.

_____ 5. Ginsburg was the best law professor at Rutgers.

_____ 6. Ruth graduated from law school at the top of her class.

_____ 7. Ruth Ginsburg was never discouraged.

_____ 8. Ginsburg won many legal battles.

Share your responses with the members of your group. Then, **identify** the paragraph where you found the information.

CAUSES AND EFFECTS

Below are a list of causes and a list of effects from the reading. Match the two.

a. Harvard Law School admitted females for the first time.

b. Ginsburg had a record of achievement in law.

c. "Ruthless Ruthie" worked hard at Columbia.

d. Ruth's parents encouraged her to be ambitious.

e. Racial and sex discrimination closed many doors.

_____ Ruth couldn't find a job as a law clerk.

_____ Ruth was a successful student.

_____ Ruth was accepted to Harvard Law School.

_____ Ginsburg graduated at the top of her class.

_____ Ruth was appointed to the U.S. Supreme Court.

Listen and Scan

Listen to these paragraphs from the reading. **Scan** each paragraph while you listen. Then, **identify** the main idea, paragraph number, and line.

Main Idea

_____

_____

Paragraph _____   Line ____

Main Idea

_____

_____

Paragraph _____   Line ____

Main Idea

_____

_____

Paragraph _____   Line ____

Notice the position of the main ideas in these paragraphs. Where is the main idea in each paragraph?

Now that you have identified the main ideas, **find** the details that support them.

Write the paragraph numbers in the column on the left. Then, **list** the details that support the main idea in each paragraph.

Paragraph   **Supporting Details**

_____   _____

Paragraph   **Supporting Details**

_____   _____

Paragraph   **Supporting Details**

_____   _____

WORD WATCH

Some of the vocabulary in the reading may be new to you.
Find synonyms for each of the words below in the numbered paragraphs.

Word	Paragraph	Synonym	Part of Speech
1. urged	2	_____	_____
2. supporter	3	_____	_____
3. excelled	5	_____	_____
4. discrimination	7	_____	_____
5. frustration	7	_____	_____

With your class or in groups, **identify the part of speech** of each word.

MATCHING

Match the **adjectives** on the left from the reading with the **nouns** that they describe on the right. **Find** the paragraphs in which these words occur.

Paragraph	Noun Match		
____	_____	1. equal	a. school
____	_____	2. strongest	b. opportunities
____	_____	3. all-male	c. rights
____	_____	4. racial	d. attitude
____	_____	5. determined	e. supporter
____	_____	6. limited	f. discrimination

Positives and Negatives

Make a list of words from the reading that describe Ruth Bader Ginsburg.
Identify the words as positive**(+)** or negative**(-) by circling the appropriate symbol.**

_____ + - _____ + -
_____ + - _____ + -
_____ + - _____ + -

Ruth Bader Ginsburg's classmates at law school gave her a nickname that indicated she never gave up. She worked very hard as a student, as a law professor, and as a lawyer.

In what areas of your life do you work hardest?

List a few of the areas below. Now **number** them in importance from where you make the greatest effort (1) to where you make the least effort (5).

____   _____

____   _____

____   _____

____   _____

____   _____

Reading this list, what do you think is the most important area of your life?

Discussion Questions/ Reading Journal Topics

1. Who does Ruth Bader Ginsburg remind you of in your family or community?

2. What do you have in common with Ginsburg?

3. What question would you like to ask this woman?

4. What do you think is the most important adjective that describes her?

CESAR CHAVEZ

"No matter what happened, I learned."

PREREADING

What were the important learning moments in your life? Did these happen at home, in school, or with your friends?

Circle any "learning moments" that apply to you.

At Home	At Work	At School	With My Friends	At Church	With My Family

Look at the picture of this famous activist. Where do you think he learned how to fight for his beliefs? What are you willing to fight for?

List the people or causes that matter to you.

1. _____

2. _____

3. _____

CESAR CHAVEZ: LEARN FROM EVERY EXPERIENCE

1   When young Cesar Chavez arrived in California, he was angry. He was only ten years old, but he was old enough to know that his family should not have to live in an aluminum shack. This shack, built for migrant workers, had no running water, no bathroom, and only one dirty room for eight people. Cesar did not act on his anger, however, until many years later, when he organized the farm workers of California to fight for better working conditions. In the years between, Cesar worked hard and learned.

2   Cesar Chavez had come with his family from Yuma, Arizona, where his grandfather had owned a ranch. The life in Yuma was not easy. There was hard work every day for both parents and children, but there was also plenty to eat, and the Chavez family was proud of working on their own land.

3   Then in 1937, the government decided to tax the farm owners. This was during the Great Depression in the United States, a time of great poverty and hardship. Families who could not pay the taxes on their property had to give their land back to the govenment. This happened to the Chavez family. They left Arizona for the promise of a better life in California.

4   However, when the Chavez family arrived in the Imperial Valley, the great agricultural center of California, they felt very discouraged. Not only was the housing terrible, but the working conditions were also unfair. With eight mouths to feed, there were no choices: they had to accept "stoop labor," picking vegetables, fruit, or cotton on farms throughout the valley and moving to a new location when a crop was finished. The pay was very low, and many times the contractors paid the workers less money than they had promised.

5   With little knowledge of English and no education, the workers had no choice: they had to accept what the contractors gave them. Cesar, a thin ten-year-old boy, had no choice, either, but he did learn from this experience. He promised himself that he would some day help his people.

6   By the time Cesar graduated from the eighth grade, he had already attended thirty-seven different schools. Even though his parents tried to stay in one place, at least during the winter, their money did not last, and they had to move on to the next crop. For Cesar, for his brothers and sisters, and for all children of migrant farm workers, these moves limited their education. How much can you learn in the classroom if the classroom changes every season?

7   Luckily for Cesar, he learned from every experience outside of the classroom. So, even though his English was never perfect, he learned from his work in the fields and from what he saw every day. Cesar went on to become the greatest labor leader in the state of California. He fought for better conditions so that workers would not get sick from the pesticides used on the crops. He fought for better pay so that families could save money and stay in one place during the school year. He fought for better living conditions for the migrant workers so that their families could live in dignity.

8   In 1959, Chavez and his wife, Helen, formed an organization called the NFWA (National Farm Workers Association) to organize the farm workers of the San Joaquin Valley. Other American workers had unions to defend their rights: truck drivers, teachers, auto workers, plumbers. Chavez believed that the farm workers, who had helped to make California one of the richest agricultural areas on earth, needed a union, too. Soon they had a flag: a white circle on red, with the black Aztec eagle in the middle.

 Times changed. The NFWA became the UFWA–the United Farm Workers of America. In 1974, California Governor Jerry Brown signed a Bill of Rights for farm workers, giving migrant workers the right to organize and fight for their rights. Still, Cesar Chavez never stopped learning and working for his people. When he died in 1993, his name had become a legend.

LISTEN AND SCAN

Listen to the questions on the tape. Stop the tape after each question. Scan for information, and write your answers on the lines below.

1. Why did the Chavez family come to California?
2. Why did the migrant families move so often?
3. What did Chavez want for migrant workers?
4. What was the name of the union that Chavez founded?

Paragraph	Line	Response
1. _____	____	_____
		_____
2. _____	____	_____
		_____
3. _____	____	_____
		_____
4. _____	____	_____
		_____

PUTTING THINGS IN ORDER

These sentences describe events in the life of Cesar Chavez.

Work with your partner to find the events in the reading.
Underline those sentences.
Then, number the paraphrases from 1 to 10, in chronological order.

_____ The NFWA was formed.

_____ The Chavez family had to give their land in Arizona to the government.

_____ Cesar graduated from the eighth grade.

_____ Governor Jerry Brown signed into law the Bill of Rights for farm workers.

_____ Cesar and his family had to live in an aluminum shack.

_____ The NFWA designed a flag with an eagle in the middle.

_____ Cesar Chavez' grandfather owned a ranch in Yuma, Arizona.

_____ The Chavez family arrived in the Imperial Valley.

_____ The National Farm Workers Association became the UFWA: The United Farm Workers of America.

_____ The Chavez family picked fruit, vegetables, and cotton.

Where did you find the sentence?
Beginning with Sentence 1, identify the paragraph and line.

Sentence	Paragraph	Line	Sentence	Paragraph	Line

List three adjectives that describe Cesar Chavez.

1. _____

2. _____

3. _____

Share your adjectives with the members of your group.

Now work as a group to analyze the following:

What did Cesar do?   Paragraph   What does this tell us about him?

_____

_____

_____

_____

_____

_____

What did Chavez say?

_____

_____

Look at your adjectives at the top of the page. Can you support them with sentences from the reading? What paragraph? What line?

Adjective	Paragraph	Line
1. _____	_____	_____
2. _____	_____	_____

INTERPRETATION

False Statements

The following statements about the reading are **incorrect**. **Find** the words that make the statements incorrect and cross them out. **Replace** the incorrect words with the appropriate words from the reading.

Share your responses with the members of your group. Then, **identify** the paragraph where you found the information. **Write** the number of the paragraph on the line before each statement.

_____ 1. Chavez signed a Bill of Rights for farm workers.

_____ 2. Cesar traveled with his family from New Mexico to California.

_____ 3. The young Cesar learned English quickly and easily.

_____ 4. The UFWA was formed in 1959.

_____ 5. By the time Cesar graduated from high school, he had attended thirty-seven different schools.

_____ 6. When he arrived in California, Cesar was a contented child.

_____ 7. Cesar Chavez learned everything he knew about life in the classroom.

_____ 8. Cesar's family left Arizona because they were starving.

CAUSES AND EFFECTS

Below are a list of causes and a list of effects from the reading. Match the two.

a. The Chavez family couldn't pay the taxes on their Arizona property.

b. Cesar's family had to move frequently.

c. Chavez worked tirelessly for the rights of the farm workers.

d. There was no running water in the small aluminum shack.

e. Working conditions were unfair.

_____ Cesar attended more than thirty different schools.

_____ His name became a legend.

_____ The Chavez family felt discouraged.

_____ Cesar and his family moved to the Imperial Valley.

_____ The young Cesar was angry.

Listen and Scan

Listen to these paragraphs from the reading. **Scan** each paragraph while you listen. Then, **identify** the main idea, paragraph number, and line.

Main Idea

_____

_____

Paragraph _____   Line ___

Main Idea

_____

_____

Paragraph _____   Line ___

Main Idea

_____

_____

Paragraph _____   Line ___

Notice the position of the main ideas in these paragraphs. Where are the main ideas located? Now that you have identified the main ideas, **find** the details that support them. **Write** the paragraph numbers in the column on the left. Then **list** the details that support the main idea in each paragraph.

Paragraph   **Supporting Details**

_____   _____

Paragraph   **Supporting Details**

_____   _____

Paragraph   **Supporting Details**

_____   _____

WORD WATCH

Some of the vocabulary in the reading may be new to you. In the groups of words below, **circle** the **one** word that does not belong in the group. Then, **share** your results with your group.

In and Out

1.	hardship	dignity	poverty
2.	US	NFWA	UFWA
3.	organization	legend	union
4.	pesticides	truck drivers	teachers
5.	angry	better	discouraged
6.	property	land	conditions

With your class or in groups, **identify the part of speech** of each group of words and **discuss** why each word you chose does **not** fit.

Opposites

In the numbered paragraphs, **find** the words that are the **opposite** of the words listed below. Then, **write** the opposite words on the blank lines.

1. Paragraph 4   cheerful   _____

2. Paragraph 7   worse   _____

3. Paragraph 2   ashamed   _____

4. Paragraph 3   riches   _____

5. Paragraph 4   wonderful   _____

6. Paragraph 5   similar   _____

7. Paragraph 6   stays the same   _____

8. Paragraph 4   fair   _____

Positives and Negatives

Make a list of words from the reading that describe Cesar Chavez. **Identify** the words as positive **(+)** or negative **(-)** by **circling the appropriate symbol.**

_____   +   -   _____   +   -

_____   +   -   _____   +   -

Cesar Chavez was an activist in the state of California. He worked hard for what he believed in, and he organized people to make changes. What are some of the changes that Chavez worked for?

List some of those changes below.

Are there any changes that you would like to make in **your** community?
List some of your changes below.
Now **number** the changes in both lists, from most important (1) to least important (4).

Chavez' Changes	**My Changes**
____ _____	____ _____
____ _____	____ _____
____ _____	____ _____
____ _____	____ _____

Discussion Questions/ Reading Journal Topics

1. Do you know any **activists** in your neighborhood or community? What changes are they working for?

2. What do you have in common with Cesar Chavez?

3. Why do you think Chavez was successful?

4. What is one change you would like to work for in school?

GUADALUPE QUINTANILLA,
RUTH BADER GINSBURG, AND CESAR CHAVEZ

Three Lives: Quintanilla, Bader Ginsburg, and Chavez

PREREADING

All of these people believed in hard work, achievement, and fighting for the rights of others. What do **you** have in common with these people? **Circle any areas that apply to you.**

Female	Latino (a)	Interest In Helping Others

Close Family	Community Service

Look at the pictures above. What adjectives describe these three people?

List your adjectives below.

1. _____

2. _____

3. _____

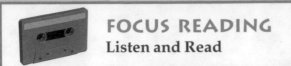
THREE LIVES: QUINTANILLA, BADER GINSBURG, AND CHAVEZ

Fitting In Information
In which paragraphs do the following sentences belong?

FOCUS READING ONE

Listen and **read** the following sentences with details about Quintanilla. Be ready to **share** your information about your focus person with your group.

Guadalupe Quintanilla: A Successful Journey

1. Her children's teachers told her that they were slow learners, but the real problem was that they could not read English.

    Paragraph ____

2. When Lupe was a little girl in Mexico, she used to read books to her grandfather, who had problems with his eyes.

    Paragraph ____

3. Lupe and the other Spanish-speaking students were not allowed to speak Spanish in school.

    Paragraph ____

4. At Texas Southmost, Lupe often got up at 4:00 a.m. to study before the rest of the family woke up.

    Paragraph ____

5. After receiving her Master of Arts degree at the University of Houston, Quintanilla was hired to teach there.

    Paragraph ____

6. Dr. Quintanilla was very concerned about keeping children in school.

    Paragraph ____

7. After receiving her Doctor of Education degree, Guadalupe was hired as the first female Hispanic administrator at the University of Houston.

    Paragraph ____

8. For eight weeks, police officers take classes to learn "street Spanish" and understand cultural differences.

    Paragraph ____

Fitting In Informaton
In which paragraphs do the following sentences belong?

FOCUS READING TWO

Listen and **read** the following sentences with details about Bader Ginsburg. Be ready to **share** your information about your focus person with your group.

Ruth Bader Ginsburg, Ruthless Ruthie: First In Her Class

1. At this time–in the 1960s–there were still many jobs that were reserved for men.

    Paragraph _____

2. Later in life, Ruth said that her mother was the strongest person she had ever known.

    Paragraph _____

3. Later, she was the first woman to be hired as a law professor at Columbia Law School.

    Paragraph _____

4. For example, the dean of the law school told Ruth that she was taking a place away from a qualified man.

    Paragraph _____

5. Although Ruth sent out dozens of applications, she had only two interviews. No one offered her a job.

    Paragraph _____

6. Ginsburg taught at Rutgers for nine years.

    Paragraph _____

7. She was very concerned about equal pay for equal work.

    Paragraph _____

8. Even though she had graduated at the top of her class in law school, the law firms were not interested in her skills.

    Paragraph _____

Fitting In Information

In which paragraphs do the following sentences belong?

FOCUS READING THREE

Listen and **read** the following sentences with details about Chavez. Be ready to **share** your information about your focus person with your group.

Cesar Chavez: "No Matter What Happened, I Learned."

1. The farm workers had to bend over all day long picking the crops, so their backs hurt.

    Paragraph ____

2. Even during the school year, Cesar and his brothers and sisters worked with their parents in the fields on the weekends.

    Paragraph ____

3. For example, Cesar learned how to take care of the grapevines in the vineyards.
    Paragraph ____

4. Although he was soft-spoken and kind, Cesar was not afraid to stand up for what he believed.

    Paragraph ____

5. Cesar and Helen worked hard to encourage people to join the union.
    Paragraph ____

6. In Yuma, the Chavez children grew up surrounded by a loving family of aunts, uncles, and cousins.

    Paragraph ____

7. Although the treatment from the contractors was unfair, there was nothing that the workers could do.

    Paragraph ____

8. Looking at the union flag, Chavez said, "To me it looks like a strong, beautiful sign of hope."

    Paragraph ____

PUTTING THINGS IN ORDER

Sharing Information:
Each person in your group has read and listened to information about **one** of the focus people. Take turns sharing your information. In your own words, tell your group members the new information you have learned.

The sentences on the first three pages of this chapter give details about the three lives: Quintanilla, Bader Ginsburg, and Chavez. These details are **not** in chronological order. Where do these details fit in the readings on these three people?

Work with your group members to find the paragraphs where each of these details fit in the readings in Chapters 1, 2, and 3. Then, write the **paragraph number** next to each of the detail sentences.

Now enter this information on the grid below:

	QUINTANILLA Paragraph	BADER GINSBURG Paragraph	CHAVEZ Paragraph
Sentence 1			
Sentence 2			
Sentence 3			
Sentence 4			
Sentence 5			
Sentence 6			
Sentence 7			
Sentence 8			

Look back at the three adjectives you listed at the beginning of the chapter. Can you support these adjectives? Fill in the grid below, using information from the first three chapters.

1   **Adjective:** _____   **What did he/she do?**

   Quintanilla   _____

   Bader Ginsburg _____

   Chavez   _____

2   **Adjective:** _____

   Quintanilla   _____

   Bader Ginsburg _____

   Chavez   _____

3   **Adjective:** _____

   Quintanilla   _____

   Bader Ginsburg _____

   Chavez   _____

Share and compare your information with the members of your group.

Can You Prove It?

The following statements are **similarities and differences**. Some of the statements you can prove (or support) from the readings in the first three chapters. Other statements can not be proven from the readings.

If you think that the readings support the statement, write **Yes** in the box. Then give the page and paragraph numbers to support the statement. If you can't prove the statement, write **No.**

Page   Paragraph   Yes/No   Statement

_____ _____ _____ 1. Both Quintanilla and Chavez grew up in large families.

_____ _____ _____ 2. Both Quintanilla and Bader Ginsburg graduated from college.

_____ _____ _____ 3. Both Bader Ginsburg and Chavez worked hard for human rights.

_____ _____ _____ 4. Cesar was born in the United States, but Lupe was born in Mexico.

_____ _____ _____ 5. Both Guadalupe and Ruth had strong, supportive mothers.

_____ _____ _____ 6. Both Guadalupe and Ruth were appointed to important positions by U.S. presidents.

_____ _____ _____ 7. Both Quintanilla and Chavez were community organizers, but Chavez worked in California, while Quintanilla worked in Texas.

_____ _____ _____ 8. Lupe loved elementary school, but Cesar did not enjoy school.

Share your responses with the members of your group. Do you agree?

Listen to the following statements. Stop the tape after each sentence. Who is the statement about–Guadalupe Quintanilla, Ruth Bader Ginsburg, or Cesar Chavez? Mark an **X** in the appropriate box on the chart. Listen more than once if necessary. Use your book to help you.

Sentence	Quintanilla	Bader Ginsburg	Chavez
1			
2			
3			
4			
5			
6			
7			

WORD WATCH

Below are some of the adjectives from the first three chapters. Work with a partner to find each adjective. Identify the adjectives by chapter and paragraph number. Then use the adjective in a new sentence of your own.

Adjective	Chapter	Paragraph	New Sentence
1. determined	_____	_____	_____ _____
2. expressive	_____	_____	_____ _____
3. discouraged	_____	_____	_____ _____
4. contented	_____	_____	_____ _____
5. ambitious	_____	_____	_____ _____
6. soft-spoken	_____	_____	_____ _____

Suffixes:
There are many posssible endings for **nouns** (persons, places, things, and ideas) in English. One common ending is **-tion**. **Working with your group members**, take one of the three chapters each and see how many nouns with this ending you can find. Then, find the nouns below. **Identify the nouns by page number and paragraph number.**

Word	Page	Paragraph
conditions	_____	_____
graduation	_____	_____
discrimination	_____	_____
location	_____	_____
communication	_____	_____

Guadalupe Quintanilla has made her mark in the field of education. Ruth Bader Ginsburg has been successful in law. Cesar Chavez was a political organizer and labor leader. Think about possible areas of success in your life. If you could do anything you wanted, what would **you** succeed in? **List** a few possibilities below. Now **number** the possibilities, from the most realistic (1) to the least realistic (4).

_____   _____

_____   _____

_____   _____

_____   _____

Reading this list, what do you think is the most important area of your life?

Discussion Questions/ Reading Journal Topics

1. Why do you think these three leaders were so successful? Choose one or two words to describe all three.

2. What similarities do they have?

3. Which person do **you** identify with? Why?

4. In what ways are **you** similar to one or all of these people?

COLIN POWELL

"Be ready for opportunity when it comes."

PREREADING

Have you had any special opportunities in your life? In what areas?

Circle any areas of opportunity that apply to you.

Jobs	**Travel**	**School**	**Sports**

Look at the picture above. What opportunities do you think this man has had?

List three opportunities in your life, in order of importance.

1. _____

2. _____

3. _____

COLIN POWELL: BE READY FOR OPPORTUNITY

1   The year is 1997. Colin Powell, speaking at the graduation ceremony of Morehouse College's School of Medicine, talked about his commitment to excellence. For him, it has been a lifelong commitment. Powell knows that in the United States, the only possible road to success–for him and for the students in the audience–is excellence. He believes that excellence is possible, and he encourages the graduating students to be ready for the future.

2   From Colin Powell, these words are filled with meaning. These words are the story of his rise, from a child of immigrant parents, to one of the most powerful positions in the nation. He has proven that success is a goal which can be achieved by the nonwhite children of immigrants. He believes, in his words, in "this wonderful country of ours."

3   Powell's parents were immigrants from the island of Jamaica. Even though they never graduated from high school, like many immigrant parents, they had high hopes for their children, and they encouraged their ambitions. They believed in the value of hard work, and they instilled this belief in Colin. Although his elementary and high school years were not outstanding (at one point, Colin was placed in a class for "slow learners"), Powell found his place at the City College of New York in the Reserve Officers' Training Corps (ROTC).

4   For the rest of his life, Colin Powell achieved success in the military. At the end of his career, he was a four-star general and Chairman of the

Joint Chiefs of Staff, the most powerful military position in the nation. As Powell, himself, has stated, there was less racial discrimination in the military than in business. He had chosen his specialty well.

5   Powell served in almost every possible position in the U.S. Army: soldier, military advisor, Major, Assistant to the Deputy Director of Management and Budget, Major General, Senior Military Advisor to the White House, National Security Advisor, Four-Star General and, finally, Chairman of the Joint Chiefs of Staff. In every position, the comments about Powell were the same: intelligent, efficient, and a good decision-maker.

6   Everyone depended on Powell: his army troops in the field, the President of the United States and all the members of the Joint Chiefs of Staff. He helped to make decisions during the Vietnam War and the Gulf War. The Army troops in the field and the people of the United States depended on him to make decisions which would support them. He earned the respect of everyone he worked with.

7   Sometimes, it was hard for Powell to remember his rise to the top. He had become one of the most respected men in the country. People were even mentioning his name as a possible presidential candidate. But just thirty years earlier, in the 1960s, Powell couldn't eat a meal in a restaurant in Fort Benning, Georgia, because of his color. Racial discrimination was one of the obstacles that he faced throughout his

youth. However, Colin Powell never made excuses for himself. He always expected the same standard of achievement. He worked hard for success.

One of the keys to Powell's success is his dedication. When he was working at the White House, Powell kept a careful schedule: he arrived at work at 6:30 in the morning and frequently didn't leave his office until 7:00 at night. Despite long hours on the job, he found time to be with his wife and three children. He recognized the importance of family life. Perhaps a friend's description of Powell is the most accurate summary of this man's character: "tough-as-nails military man" with "compassion and soul." Colin Powell is a model for us all.

LISTEN AND SCAN

Listen to the questions on the tape. Stop the tape after each question. Scan for information, and write your answers on the lines below.

1. Where were Powell's parents born?
2. What kind of student was Colin in high school?
3. What happened in Fort Benning, Georgia?
4. What was Powell's highest office in the military?

	Paragraph	Line	Response
1.	_____	___	_____
2.	_____	___	_____
3.	_____	___	_____
4.	_____	___	_____

PUTTING THINGS IN ORDER

The sentences below are **paraphrases**. A paraphrase is a sentence with the same meaning as another sentence, but using different words.

Work with your partner to find the sentences in the reading with the same meaning. Underline those sentences.
Then, number the paraphrases from 1 to 10, in the order in which they occur in the reading.

_____ Some people thought that Colin Powell should run for president.

_____ Powell served in the Reserve Officers Training Corps in New York.

_____ Colin Powell believes that family life is important.

_____ At the White House, Powell worked long hours.

_____ Powell wasn't allowed to eat in a restaurant in Fort Benning, Georgia.

_____ In the early years of his education, Colin was not a good student.

_____ All of Powell's coworkers respected him.

_____ Powell achieved his goals by working hard.

_____ Powell believes that excellence is necessary for success.

_____ Colin Powell had several different positions in the military.

Where did you find the sentence?
Beginning with Sentence 1, identify the paragraph and line.

Sentence	Paragraph	Line	Sentence	Paragraph	Line
_____	_____	_____	_____	_____	_____
_____	_____	_____	_____	_____	_____
_____	_____	_____	_____	_____	_____
_____	_____	_____	_____	_____	_____

List three adjectives that describe Colin Powell.

1. _____

2. _____

3. _____

Share your adjectives with the members of your group.
Now work as a group to analyze the following:

What did Powell do?	Paragraph	What does this tell us about Powell?

What did Powell say?

_____

_____

Look at your adjectives at the top of the page. Can you support them with sentences from the reading? What paragraph? What line?

	Adjective	Paragraph	Line
1.	_____	_____	_____
2.	_____	_____	_____
3.	_____	_____	_____

False Statements

The following statements about the reading are **incorrect**. **Find** the words that make the statements incorrect and cross them out. **Replace** the incorrect words with the appropriate words from the reading.
Share your responses with the members of your group. Then, **identify** the paragraph where you found the information. **Write** the number of the paragraph on the line before each statement.

___ 1. Colin Powell was an immigrant from Jamaica.

___ 2. Powell helped to make military decisions during World War II.

___ 3. Powell kept a regular, nine-to-five schedule in the White House.

___ 4. Racial discrimination never affected Colin Powell.

___ 5. Colin was an excellent student in elementary school.

___ 6. Some people wanted Powell to run for vice president.

___ 7. Colin Powell served in three positions in the U.S. military.

___ 8. Although Powell's parents never attended college, both were high school graduates.

CAUSES AND EFFECTS

Below are a list of causes and a list of effects from the reading. Match the two.

a. Powell is an African-American.

b. The President and the Joint Chiefs of Staff depended on Powell.

c. Powell was successful in the ROTC Program at City College in New York.

d. Colin Powell was a good decision-maker.

e. Powell's parents believed in the value of hard work.

___ Colin Powell believes in working hard.

___ Powell served in the military.

___ Some people wanted Powell to run for U.S. President.

___ In the 1960s, Powell couldn't eat in a Georgia restaurant.

___ Powell earned the respect of everyone he worked with.

Listen and Scan

Listen to these paragraphs from the reading. **Scan** the paragraphs while you listen. Then, **identify** the main idea, paragraph number, and line.

Main Idea

_____

_____

Paragraph _____   Line ___

Main Idea

_____

_____

Paragraph _____   Line ___

Main Idea

_____

_____

Paragraph _____   Line ___

Notice the position of the main ideas in these paragraphs. Is the main idea always in the same place in each paragraph?

Now that you have identified the main ideas, **find** the details that support them. **Write** the paragraph numbers in the column on the left. Then, **list** the details that support the main idea in each paragraph.

Paragraph   **Supporting Details**

_____   _____

Paragraph   **Supporting Details**

_____   _____

Paragraph   **Supporting Details**

_____   _____

Some of the vocabulary in the reading may be new to you. Find **synonyms** (words that mean the same) for the nouns below in the numbered paragraphs. **Underline** the word in the reading. Then, **identify** the noun ending. Work with your classmates to find a synonym for each word.

Word	Paragraph	Noun Ending	Synonym
1. excellence	1	_____	_____
2. ambitions	3	_____	_____
3. discrimination	4	_____	_____
4. achievement	7	_____	_____
5. importance	8	_____	_____

MATCHING

Match the words on the left with their synonyms on the right. Both sets of words are in the reading. **Find** the paragraphs in which these words occur. **Write** the paragraph numbers below.

Paragraph	Synonym			Paragraph
____	_____	1. commitment	a. value	____
____	_____	2. achieved	b. hopes	____
____	_____	3. ambitions	c. know	____
____	_____	4. recognize	d. excellent	____
____	_____	5. importance	e. earned	____
____	_____	6. outstanding	f. dedication	____

Which words on these lists are **nouns**? How do you know?

Which words are **verbs**? (Words that describe what Powell did.)

Which words are **adjectives**? (Words that describe a person.)

Colin Powell believes in opportunity. He believes that we need to be ready for new possibilities in our lives. Where will **your** opportunities be: in education, in sports, in business, in the military?

List some of the opportunities in Powell's life.
Then, **list** some of the opportunities in your life.
Now **number** the opportunities in both lists, from the most important (1) to the least important (4).

	In Powell's Life		In My Life
____	_____	____	_____
____	_____	____	_____
____	_____	____	_____
____	_____	____	_____

Discussion Questions/ Reading Journal Topics

1. Why has Colin Powell been so successful?

2. What do you have in common with Powell? Does Powell remind you of anyone you know in your family or community?

4. Is there anything you would like to ask Colin Powell?

PATSY TAKEMOTO MINK

Patsy Takemoto Mink: "Don't take 'No' for an answer."

PREREADING

Look at the picture above. Can you tell from Patsy Mink's face that she is not easily discouraged? What do her words, "Don't take 'No' for an answer" mean?
In what areas of your life do you sometimes feel discouraged?
Circle any areas that apply to you.

School	Family Relationships	Work	Sports	Community Relationships

When you feel discouraged, who do you talk to? What do you do to help yourself feel better? Where do you go to get help?

List your sources of strength below.

1. _____
2. _____
3. _____

PATSY TAKEMOTO MINK: "DON'T TAKE 'NO' FOR AN ANSWER

1   If you looked at Patsy Mink's life from the outside, you might think it was easy. She grew up in Hawaii, a beautiful place for a little girl to learn and grow. Her father was an engineer, and her family did not have to worry a lot about money. But many things happened in Patsy's life which made challenges for her. Despite her middle-class background and her comfortable family life, she faced many obstacles. There were many "No's" in her life, even before she graduated from high school. Patsy had to learn to face challenges.

2   Patsy's earliest challenges were in school. The normal age for children to begin school in Hawaii was five, but Patsy wanted to begin at four. Why? Maybe she knew she needed to learn to fight, and she wanted to get an early start! Later, she decided to attend the American Kaunoa English Standard School, which did not usually accept nonwhite students. Patsy was accepted, but her years at Kaunoa were lonely, and she had to travel a long way to school. Determined little Patsy used her free time to read and listen to the radio. She was getting ready for her future.

3   Patsy's school days became more difficult during World War II. After Japan bombed Pearl Harbor, the attitude toward Japanese-Americans in Hawaii became very negative. Even though they were loyal citizens, Japanese-Americans were often mistreated. In Hawaii, at least, these citizens were not placed in internment camps as they were on the mainland. But the children were isolated and insulted at school.

4   Patsy tried not to be discouraged. She was, by nature, a very positive person, and this helped her to live through those difficult years. She also had many interests. She kept her spirits up by "doing her own thing." Science was always one of her best subjects in school. In her spare time, Patsy worked on her plant and insect collections. She also loved to dance, especially the Hawaiian Hula. She enjoyed the natural beauty and culture of Hawaii.

5 After Patsy transferred to Maui High School, she felt more at home. She developed an interest in politics and was elected student body president. When she graduated from high school, she was class valedictorian. Deciding that she wanted to study medicine, she enrolled at the University of Hawaii and was president of the Pre-medical Students Club. It seemed that Patsy had finally found her place.

6 However, several years later, graduating from college, Patsy ran into another obstacle. She had applied to several different medical schools but was not accepted by any. She had a boring, low-paying job as a clerk-typist in a small museum. Was this why she had gone to college?

7 Then a casual conversation with a friend changed Patsy's life. The friend suggested that since she had always been interested in politics, she should think about a career in lawmaking. Soon she was admitted to law school at the University of Chicago. This career choice changed her life.

8 After Patsy passed the bar exam in Hawaii several years later, she started her own law practice. Her positive attitude and her appreciation of the culture and people of Hawaii gave her an interest in politics which continued for the rest of her life. She became first a

representative and then a senator in the Hawaiian legislature, where she was known as a champion of the underdog. In 1965, Takemoto Mink was elected to the U.S. Congress, the first Asian-American woman to hold this position.

 For the next thirty years, Patsy's interest in politics continued, but her career was marked by ups and downs. Although she lost many political battles, her basic optimism and concern for people remained. She fought for her beliefs, even when they were unpopular, and has kept the respect of her people and her colleagues.

LISTEN AND SCAN

Listen to the questions on the tape. Stop the tape after each question. Scan for information, and write your answers on the lines below.

1. Why didn't Patsy go to medical school?

2. What happened in 1965?

3. How did Patsy keep up her spirits in childhood?

4. Where did Takemoto Mink attend law school?

Paragraph	Line	Response
1. _____	____	_____
		_____
2. _____	____	_____
		_____
3. _____	____	_____
		_____
4. _____	____	_____
		_____

PUTTING THINGS IN ORDER

The sentences below describe events in Patsy Takemoto Mink's life.
Work with your partner to find the events in the reading. Underline those sentences. Then number the sentences from 1 to 10, in chronological order.

_____ Patsy transferred to Maui High School.

_____ Takemoto Mink passed the bar exam in Hawaii.

_____ During World War II, Japanese-American children were insulted in school.

_____ Patsy was not accepted by any medical schools.

_____ Mink became a representative in the Hawaiian legislature.

_____ Patsy decided to attend the American Kaunoa English Standard School.

_____ Patsy worked as a clerk-typist in a small museum in Hawaii.

_____ Takemoto Mink was the first Asian-American woman to be elected to the U.S. Congress.

_____ Patsy began school at the age of four.

_____ Patsy was valedictorian of her graduating class in high school.

Where did you find the sentence?

Beginning with Sentence 1, identify the paragraph and line.

Sentence	Paragraph	Line	Sentence	Paragraph	Line
_____	_____	_____	_____	_____	_____
_____	_____	_____	_____	_____	_____
_____	_____	_____	_____	_____	_____
_____	_____	_____	_____	_____	_____
_____	_____	_____	_____	_____	_____

List three adjectives that describe Patsy Takemoto Mink.

1. _____

2. _____

3. _____

Can you support your adjectives with sentences from the reading?
What paragraph? What line?

	Adjective	**Paragraph**	**Line**
1.			
2.			
3.			

Share your adjectives with the members of your group.

Now work as a group to analyze the following:

What did Mink do?	Paragraph	What does this tell us about Mink?

What events changed Mink's life?

_____

_____

Fact or Opinion?

Some of the following statements about the reading are **facts** and some are **opinions**. **Identify** which are **facts (F)** and which are **opinions (O)**. **Underline** the words in the **opinion** sentences which identify an opinion.

Share your responses with the members of your group. **Identify** the paragraph where you found the information. **Write** the number of the paragraph on the line before each statement.

_____ 1. The students at Maui High School elected Patsy as student body president.

_____ 2. Takemoto Mink is an optimistic person.

_____ 3. Patsy was not accepted to medical school because she was a female.

_____ 4. Patsy was lonely at Kaunoa English Standard School

_____ 5. Takemoto became the most popular politician in Hawaii.

_____ 6. When Patsy graduated from high school, she was first in her class.

_____ 7. Patsy never felt discouraged.

_____ 8. Patsy's positive attitude helped her during difficult years.

CAUSES AND EFFECTS

Below are a list of causes and a list of effects from the reading. Match the two.

a. Patsy wanted to study medicine.

b. Patsy decided to attend the American Kaunoa English Standard School.

c. Patsy was always interested in science.

d. Takemoto Mink passed the bar exam.

e. Mink had always been interested in politics.

_____ She started her own law practice.

_____ Mink was elected to the Hawaiian legislature.

_____ She was president of the Pre-medical Students Club.

_____ She had to travel a long way to school.

_____ Patsy collected plants and insects.

STRUCTURE ANALYSIS

Listen and Scan

Listen to these paragraphs from the reading. **Scan** the paragraph while you listen. Now underline the main idea and identify by paragraph number and line:

Main Idea

_____

_____

Paragraph _____   Line _____

Main Idea

_____

_____

Paragraph _____   Line _____

Main Idea

_____

_____

Paragraph _____   Line _____

Notice the position of the main ideas in these paragraphs. Where is the main idea in each paragraph?

Now that you have identified the main ideas, **find** the details that support them. **Write** the paragraph numbers in the column at the left. Then **list** the details that support the main idea in each paragraph.

Paragraph   **Supporting Details**

_____   _____

Paragraph   **Supporting Details**

_____   _____

Paragraph   **Supporting Details**

_____   _____

Some of the vocabulary in the reading may be new to you. In the groups of words below, **circle** the **one** word that does not fit the group. **Share** your results with your partner.

In and Out

1. colleagues	challenges	obstacles
2. isolated	discouraged	determined
3. enrolled	admitted	applied
4. senator	representative	champion
5. elected	isolated	mistreated
6. appreciation	position	interest

With your class or in groups, identify the **part of speech** of each group of words.

MATCHING

Match the **adjectives** on the left from the reading with the **nouns** that they describe on the right. **Find** the paragraphs in which these words occur. **Write** the paragraph numbers below.

Paragraph	Noun		Paragraph	Noun	
____	_____	1. determined	____	_____	a. job
____	_____	2. loyal	____	_____	b. place
____	_____	3. casual	____	_____	c. Patsy
____	_____	4. natural	____	_____	d. attitude
____	_____	5. positive	____	_____	e. citizens
____	_____	6. political	____	_____	f. conversation
____	_____	7. boring	____	_____	g. beauty
____	_____	8. beautiful	____	_____	h. battles

Positives and Negatives

Make a list of words from the reading that describe Patsy Mink. Identify these words as positive(+) or negative(-) by circling the appropriate symbol.

_____ + - _____ + -

_____ + - _____ + -

What people remember about Patsy Takemoto Mink is that she never gave up: in school, in her career, in politics. When Patsy heard the word, "no," it meant: "find another way." This is exactly what she did. When one door closed in front of her, she looked for another door. Think about your life. In what parts of your life have you faced a closed door? **List some areas of your life in which you have faced obstacles.**

_____

_____

_____

_____

_____

_____

_____

Reading this list, what do you think you can do to find "another door"? How can you make this "No" mean "find another way"?

Discussion Questions/ Reading Journal Topics

1. Think about Patsy Takemoto Mink. Who does she remind you of? Why?

2. What do you have in common with Mink?

3. What question would you like to ask this woman?

4. Which part of her life is the most impressive to you?

STEVEN SPIELBERG

"Learn to face your fears."

PREREADING

What fears did you have when you were young?
Circle any areas of fear that apply to you.

Strangers   **Monsters**   **Insects**   **"Bad Guys"**

   The Dark   **Water**   **Being Alone**

Look at the picture above. What fears do you think this man had?

List–in order of importance–three things that you are afraid of now.

1. _____

2. _____

3. _____

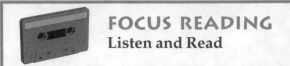
STEVEN SPIELBERG: "LEARN TO FACE YOUR FEARS."

1   Screams of horror filled the air as the great white shark broke the surface of the water. Crowds of swimmers raced to the shore in panic. This was one of many fear-filled scenes in "Jaws," one of Steven Spielberg's early successful films. Who would guess that as a child, Steven was afraid of almost everything? In learning to manage his own fears, he put them to work, building one of the most successful careers in film history.

2   Almost from the moment of his birth in 1947, Steven Spielberg was a dynamo. His mother remembers that he was never a cozy, snuggly baby. He had a lot of energy, which he learned very young to use in filmmaking. His career did not begin in his twenties or even in his teens. Steven was making films—on an 8-mm camera—at the incredible age of twelve!

3   Steven's career began on the living room floor. There he staged train wrecks with his electric trains and then filmed the action so that it looked like a life-size collision. Family members remember that the house was always full of floodlights, cables, and camera equipment. Steven's "hobby" was everywhere.

4   You might think, "This guy didn't have a tough life! His parents supported his expensive hobby. He got an early start on success." But it didn't feel that way to Steven. He worked hard at developing his hobby because he was miserable in school. Schoolwork was a challenge for Spielberg, especially math. In addition, he was a poor athlete in a school where sports were very important. Small and skinny, Steven was picked on by the school bullies, who used to chase him home from school.

Sometimes he pretended to be sick so that he could avoid the terrors of the schoolyard.

5 However, Steven had other sources of fear. He remembers that as a child, he was afraid of everything: the trees at night, the wind, even clouds! Because he had so many fears, he began to enjoy the thrill of being afraid. Eventually, in the movies he made, Spielberg shared this thrill of fear with moviegoers all over the world.

6 Before "Jaws" was released in the summer of 1975, Spielberg said that this thrilling movie was going to shake people up. He was right. When the movie was first released, it earned $100 million, the biggest success in moviemaking history. At the time, Spielberg was just 27 years old. In fifteen years, Steven had moved from the living room floor to Hollywood stardom!

7 From then on, Spielberg's successes continued. "Close Encounters of the Third Kind," another thriller, opened up the world of science fiction. "Raiders of the Lost Ark," "Poltergeist," and "E.T." soon followed. In one year, Spielberg produced both "Gremlins" and "Indiana Jones and the Temple of Doom." All of these films included supernatural challenges, special effects, and the fear of the unknown.

8 However, Spielberg was interested in trying new challenges. One of these was "The Color Purple," which he directed in 1985. In this film,

Spielberg was working with the lives of real people, with no visits from outer space and no supernatural heroes. The challenge was different: to show the pain and difficulties in the lives of real people. Spielberg had found a new direction as a film director.

Steven Spielberg found a way to put his childhood fears to use. Does that mean that he is not afraid of anything now? Spielberg states that he still has many fears. He is afraid of the ocean (maybe from "Jaws"!), roller coasters, elevators, and bugs. He is afraid of being sick and speaking in public. But Steven is not afraid of being successful. And success can be thrilling, too.

LISTEN AND SCAN
Listen to the questions on the tape. Stop the tape after each question. Scan for information, and write your answers on the lines below.

1. Where did Spielberg begin making films?

2. When Steven was young, what was he afraid of?

3. When did Spielberg direct "The Color Purple"?

4. What was the name of the first movie that made Spielberg a big success?

Paragraph	Line	Response
1. _____	____	_____
		_____
2. _____	____	_____
		_____
3. _____	____	_____
		_____
4. _____	____	_____
		_____

These sentences are **paraphrases**. A paraphrase is a sentence with the same meaning as another sentence, but using different words.

Work with your partner to find the sentences in the reading with the same meaning. Underline those sentences. Then number the paraphrases from 1 to 10, in the order in which they occur in the reading.

_____ From this time on, Spielberg was successful.

_____ His mother says that Steven wasn't cuddly as a baby.

_____ Steven had other things to be afraid of.

_____ Steven's family home was filled with his hobby equipment.

_____ Steven always wanted to try new things.

_____ School assignments, especially in math, were hard for Steven.

_____ Spielberg says that he is still afraid of many things.

_____ Because he was not happy at school, Steven spent a lot of time at home, making films.

_____ Steven's small size made him a target for bullies, who chased him home after school.

_____ Spielberg became interested in directing a different kind of film.

Where did you find the sentence?

Beginning with Sentence 1, identify the paragraph and line.

Sentence	Paragraph	Line		Sentence	Paragraph	Line
_____	_____	_____		_____	_____	_____
_____	_____	_____		_____	_____	_____
_____	_____	_____		_____	_____	_____
_____	_____	_____		_____	_____	_____
_____	_____	_____		_____	_____	_____

List three adjectives that describe Steven Spielberg.

1. _____

2. _____

3. _____

Share your adjectives with the members of your group.

Now work as a group to analyze the following:

What did Spielberg do?   Paragraph   What does this tell us about Spielberg?

_____

_____

_____

_____

_____

What did Spielberg say?

_____

_____

What did other people say about Steven Spielberg?

_____

_____

Look at your adjectives at the top of the page. Can you support them with sentences from the reading? What paragraph? What line?

Adjective	Paragraph	Line
1. _____	____	____
2. _____	____	____
3. _____	____	____

INTERPRETATION

False Statements

The following statements about the reading are **incorrect**. **Find** the words that make the statements incorrect and cross them out. **Replace** the incorrect words with words from the reading.

Share your responses with the members of your group. **Identify** the paragraph where you found the information. **Write** the number of the paragraph on the line before each statement.

_____ 1. As a baby, Steven was very relaxed and calm.

_____ 2. Spielberg began making films at the age of twenty-seven.

_____ 3. Spielberg's first film was made in Hollywood.

_____ 4. When he was young, Steven was not afraid of anything.

_____ 5. Spielberg's first big success was "The Color Purple."

_____ 6. Spielberg enjoys speaking in public.

_____ 7. "The Color Purple" was one of Spielberg's best science fiction films.

_____ 8. Steven was always good at schoolwork, especially math.

CAUSES AND EFFECTS

Below are a list of causes and a list of effects from the reading. Match the two.

a. Steven was miserable in school.

b. "Jaws" earned $100 million in its first release.

c. As a child, Steven was afraid of many things.

d. Spielberg's film career began at home.

e. Steven was interested in new challenges.

_____ The house was full of camera equipment.

_____ He decided to direct "The Color Purple."

_____ Sometimes he stayed home, pretending to be sick.

_____ It was the biggest success in film history.

_____ He began to enjoy the thrill of being afraid.

Listen and Scan
Listen to these paragraphs from the reading. **Scan** the paragraph while you listen.
Then, **identify** the main idea, paragraph number, and line.

Main Idea

_____

_____

Paragraph _____   Line _____

Main Idea

_____

_____

Paragraph _____   Line _____

Main Idea

_____

_____

Paragraph _____   Line _____

Notice the position of the main ideas in these paragraphs. Is the main idea always in the same place in the paragraph?

Now that you have identified the main ideas, **find** the details that support them. **Write** the paragraph numbers in the column on the left. Then, **list** the details that support the main idea in each paragraph.

Paragraph	Supporting Details
_____	_____
Paragraph	Supporting Details
_____	_____
Paragraph	Supporting Details
_____	_____

WORD WATCH

Some of the vocabulary in the reading may be new to you. Find **synonyms** (words that have similar meanings) for the nouns below in the numbered paragraphs. **Underline** the word in the reading. Then, **identify** the noun ending. Work with your classmates to find a synonym for each word.

	Word	Paragraph	Noun Ending	Synonym
1.	collision	3	_____	_____
2.	equipment	3	_____	_____
3.	challenge	4	_____	_____
4.	stardom	6	_____	_____
5.	direction	8	_____	_____

MATCHING

In the numbered paragraphs, find the words that are the **antonyms** (opposites) of the words listed below. **Write** the words on the lines below.

1. Paragraph 7   failures   _____
2. Paragraph 1   pleasure   _____
3. Paragraph 4   easy   _____
4. Paragraph 2   end   _____
5. Paragraph 4   happy   _____
6. Paragraph 9   private   _____
7. Paragraph 4   excellent   _____
8. Paragraph 4   late   _____

Positives and Negatives

Make a list of words from the reading that describe Steven Spielberg. Identify the words as positive(+) or negative(-) by circling the appropriate symbol.

_____   +   -   _____   +   -

_____   +   -   _____   +   -

Steven Spielberg had many fears as a child. Spielberg used his fears as a source of energy to make films.

List below some of the things that Spielberg was afraid of as a child and as an adult. Then, **list** some of your fears.

Steven's Fears	My Fears
_____	_____
_____	_____
_____	_____
_____	_____
_____	_____

Discussion Questions/ Reading Journal Topics

1. Why do you think Spielberg's movies are so successful?

2. Do you know anyone who has many fears like Steven? Who does he remind you of?

3. What do you have in common with Steven?

4. What is one adjective you would use to describe Steven Spielberg?

COLIN POWELL, PATSY TAKEMOTO MINK, AND STEVEN SPIELBERG

Three Lives: Powell, Takemoto Mink, and Spielberg

PREREADING

All of these people made good use of opportunities and worked hard to succeed.

What do **you** have in common with these people?
Circle any nouns that apply to you.

Supportive Parents   **Lots of Energy**   **Optimism**

Immigrant Family   **Determination**

Look at the pictures above. What adjectives describe these three people?
List your adjectives below.

1. _____

2. _____

3. _____

THREE LIVES: POWELL, TAKEMOTO MINK, AND SPIELBERG

Fitting In Information
In which paragraphs do the following sentences belong?

FOCUS READING ONE

Listen and **read** the following sentences with details about Powell. Be ready to **share** your information about your focus person with your group.

Colin Powell: Be Ready For Opportunity When It Comes

1. Powell says that there are no secrets to success. Success comes from hard work, persistence, and loyalty to coworkers.
   Paragraph ____

2. Colin's father was a shipping clerk, and his mother was a seamstress.
   Paragraph ____

3. Colin attended elementary and high school in the Bronx in New York City.
   Paragraph ____

4. Powell graduated from college at the top of his ROTC class.
   Paragraph ____

5. During the war in Vietnam, he received many awards, including the Purple Heart and the Bronze Medal for bravery and distinguished service.
   Paragraph ____

6. Powell was promoted from Major to Major General when Jimmy Carter was president.
   Paragraph ____

7. His nomination as Chairman to the Joint Chiefs of Staff was made in 1989 by President George Bush.
   Paragraph ____

8. Colin and Alma Powell have raised one son and two daughters.
   Paragraph ____

Fitting In Information

In which paragraphs do the following sentences belong?

FOCUS READING TWO

Listen and **read** the following sentences with details about Takemoto Mink. Be ready to **share** your information about your focus person with your group.

Patsy Takemoto Mink: Don't Take "No" For An Answer

1. Patsy was born on the Hawaiian island of Maui.

    Paragraph _____

2. Her room was full of labeled jars of plants and bugs.

    Paragraph _____

3. At the university, she was also a member of the Varsity Debate Team.

    Paragraph _____

4. At Chicago, she met John Mink, a graduate student who later became her husband.

    Paragraph _____

5. Because no law firm would hire her, Patsy decided to set up her own practice.

    Paragraph _____

6. In 1954, in her first political move, Takemoto Mink was elected president of the Young Democrats, a political group.

    Paragraph _____

7. Mink served in the U.S. Congress for six terms.

    Paragraph _____

8. During her political career, Mink was especially interested in education and child care issues.

    Paragraph _____

Fitting In Information
In which paragraphs do the following sentences belong?

FOCUS READING THREE

Listen and **read** the following sentences with details about Spielberg. Be ready to **share** your information about your focus person with your group.

Steven Spielberg: Learn To Face Your Fears

1. Steven was Leah and Arnold Spielberg's first child.

   Paragraph ____

2. The whole family dressed up in crazy costumes to act in Steven's film experiments.

   Paragraph ____

3. Steven had difficulty concentrating in the classroom, so he kept himself happy by drawing cartoons.

   Paragraph ____

4. When teams were picked to play baseball, Steven was usually the last player picked.

   Paragraph ____

5. He imagined that there were monsters under his bed and ghosts living in the crack on the wall.

   Paragraph ____

6. "The Goonies" was another Spielberg film project.

   Paragraph ____

7. The movie earned four Academy Award nominations.

   Paragraph ____

8. "The Color Purple" was followed by "Empire of the Sun," another movie which focused on the painful experiences of real people.

   Paragraph ____

Each person in your group has read and listened to information about **one** of the focus people. Take turns sharing your information. In your own words, tell your group members the new information you have learned.

PUTTING THINGS IN ORDER

The sentences on the first three pages of this chapter give details about the three lives: Powell, Takemoto Mink, and Spielberg. These details are not in chronological order. Where do these details fit in the readings on these three people?

Work with your group members to find the paragraphs where these details fit in the readings in chapters 5, 6, and 7. Then, write the **paragraph number** next to each of the detail sentences. Now enter this information on the grid below.

	POWELL Paragraph	TAKEMOTO MINK Paragraph	SPIELBERG Paragraph
Sentence 1			
Sentence 2			
Sentence 3			
Sentence 4			
Sentence 5			
Sentence 6			
Sentence 7			
Sentence 8			

Look back at the three adjectives you listed at the beginning of the chapter. Can you support these adjectives? Fill in the grid below, using information from Chapters 5, 6, and 7.

1   **Adjective:**   _____   **What did he/she do?**

      Powell   _____

      Takemoto Mink   _____

      Spielberg   _____

2   **Adjective:**   _____   **What did he/she do?**

      Powell   _____

      Takemoto Mink   _____

      Spielberg   _____

3   **Adjective:**   _____   **What did he/she do?**

      Powell   _____

      Takemoto Mink   _____

      Spielberg   _____

Share and compare your information with the members of your group.

Can You Prove It?

The following statements are **similarities and differences**. Some of the statements you can prove (or support) from the readings in chapters 5, 6, and 7. Other statements cannot be proven from the readings. If you think that the readings support the statement, write **Yes**. Then give the page and paragraph numbers to support the statement. If you can't prove the statement, write **No**.

Page	Paragraph	Yes/No	Statement
_____	_____	_____	1. Both Powell and Spielberg had supportive parents.
_____	_____	_____	2. As young boys, both Steven and Colin had many fears.
_____	_____	_____	3. Both Takemoto Mink and Powell were involved in U.S. politics.
_____	_____	_____	4. The parents of both Spielberg and Powell were immigrants.
_____	_____	_____	5. Both Powell and Takemoto suffered racial discrimination.
_____	_____	_____	6. Both Takemoto Mink and Powell went to college, but Spielberg did not.
_____	_____	_____	7. In the early years, school was difficult for both Powell and Spielberg.
_____	_____	_____	8. Steven chose his career at a young age, but Patsy made her career choice when she was older.

Share your responses with the members of your group. Do all of you agree?

MEMORY CHECK

Listen to the following statements. Stop the tape after each sentence. Who is the statement about–Colin Powell, Patsy Takemoto Mink, or Steven Spielberg? Mark an **X** in the appropriate box on the chart. Listen more than once if necessary. Use your book to help you.

Sentence	Powell	Takemoto Mink	Spielberg
1			
2			
3			
4			
5			
6			
7			

WORD WATCH

Below are some of the adjectives from chapters 5, 6, and 7. Work with a partner to find each adjective. Identify the adjectives by chapter and paragraph number. Then use the adjective in a new sentence of your own.

Adjective	Chapter	Paragraph	New Sentence
1. miserable	_____	_____	_____
			_____
2. determined	_____	_____	_____
			_____
3. powerful	_____	_____	_____
			_____
4. successful	_____	_____	_____
			_____
5. positive	_____	_____	_____
			_____
6. respected	_____	_____	_____
			_____

Suffixes:
There are many posssible endings for **nouns** (persons, places, things, and ideas) in English. One common ending is **-tion**. Working with your group members, take one of the three chapters each and see how many nouns with this ending you can find. Then, find the nouns below. Identify the nouns by page number and paragraph number.

Word	Page	Paragraph
conversation	_____	_____
dedication	_____	_____
collision	_____	_____
ambitions	_____	_____
collections	_____	_____

Colin Powell became the most powerful military leader in the country. Patsy Takemoto Mink became one of the top political leaders in Hawaii. Steven Spielberg became one of the most successful film directors in history. All three people had obstacles to overcome on the road to success. What obstacles do **you** see before you? List a few of them below. Which of these obstacles do you think will be most difficult to overcome?

_____

_____

_____

_____

Discussion Questions/ Reading Journal Topics

1. Why do you think these three leaders were so successful? Choose one or two words to describe all three.

2. What similarities do they share?

3. Which person do **you** identify with? Why?

4. In what ways are **you** similar to one or all of these people?

SHIRLEY CHISHOLM

"Fighting Shirley Chisholm"

PREREADING

Shirley Chisholm was known in politics as a fighter: for education, for childcare, for equal rights for women. What are you willing to fight for?

Circle any areas that apply to you.

    Friends   Ideas   Family Members   Civil Rights

Look at the picture above. Why do you think this woman was able to fight for the rights of other people? What strengths do you think she needed?

FIGHTING SHIRLEY CHISHOLM: UNBOUGHT AND UNBOSSED

1   When Shirley Chisholm ran for the United States Congress in 1968, her campaign slogan was "Fighting Shirley Chisholm: Unbought and Unbossed." Men, women, and children all over New York City carried shopping bags printed with this slogan. To many people, these bags symbolized the underpaid, hardworking workers who crowded the subways at night with their shopping bags. Shirley was a hero to these people and to many other voters in the city. She won the election by more than two-to-one over her opponent! "Fighting Shirley" had become the first African-American woman elected to the United States Congress.

2   Chisholm understood the lives of the people in her district. Many of these people were immigrants who worked at two and even three jobs to support their families. Although Shirley was born in Brooklyn, New York, her parents were immigrants from Barbados, an island in the Caribbean. When she was very young, Shirley and her two younger sisters were sent back to Barbados to live with their grandmother so that both of the parents could work. Shirley didn't return to New York until she was ten years old, so in many ways she was an immigrant, too!

3   The seven years in Barbados were important years for Shirley. Living on the grandmother's farm, the girls had many advantages. They enjoyed the beautiful flowers and fruits of the island, as well as daily swims in the sparkling blue Caribbean. Because there were many chores on the farm, Shirley and her sisters also learned to work at a young age.

4   The return to New York City was a mixed experience. Shirley was with her parents again, but she encountered racism for the first time. She couldn't get used to the hateful names the white and black children called one another or the fights that followed the name-calling. In addition, Shirley, who had always been a good student, was moved from the sixth grade class down to the third grade because she hadn't studied American history and geography. She felt ashamed and, as a result, acted up in class. Shirley was on her way to becoming a problem student!

5   Luckily, a teacher realized that Shirley was not the problem. She was moved back to the sixth grade and soon learned the facts about the United States that she needed in that grade. From then on, Chisholm excelled in school. Instead of a problem, she became a star.

6   However, that time of adjustment was important for Shirley Chisholm. She learned to be a fighter. Years later, when she became interested in politics, she was known as a "troublemaker" because she would not accept unequal status in the Democratic Party for women or for African-Americans. When she decided to run for the New York State Assembly in 1963, many people tried to discourage her. They still believed that women should stay at home and that African-Americans should not be leaders. Shirley paid no attention. Because of her hard work in her political district, she won the election easily.

7   When Chisholm was elected to the United States House of Representatives, she continued to be known as a fighter. Even in her "freshman" year in Congress, Shirley was outspoken and vocal. She was especially concerned about education, the daycare needs of working women, and equal rights for women in general. One of the many bills which she introduced in the House was one to give maids and domestic

workers a minimum wage. She didn't forget the people who had first elected her.

 Shirley Chisholm was a member of Congress for fifteen years. In 1972, she ran for president of the United States. Even though she did not win the Democratic nomination, she put up a good fight. After she left the House of Representatives, she went on to become a professor of government at Mount Holyoke College. Chisholm never stopped working for the causes she believed in.

LISTEN AND SCAN
Listen to the questions on the tape. Stop the tape after each question. Scan for information, and write your answers on the lines below.

1. Where were Chisholm's parents born?

2. When Shirley moved back to New York, what bothered her?

3. What happened in 1963?

4. How long did Chisholm serve in the House of Representatives?

	Paragraph	Line	Response
1.	_____	___	_____
			_____
2.	_____	___	_____
			_____
3.	_____	___	_____
			_____
4.	_____	___	_____
			_____

PUTTING THINGS IN ORDER

The sentences below are **paraphrases**. A paraphrase is a sentence with the same meaning as another sentence, but using different words.

Work with your partner to find the sentences in the reading with the same meaning. Underline those sentences.
Then, number the paraphrases from 1 to 10, in the order in which they occur in the reading.

_____ There were many benefits to life on the farm in Barbados.

_____ From that time on, Shirley was one of the best students.

_____ Shirley always worked hard for her beliefs.

_____ Shirley was the champion of many people in New York City.

_____ Shirley spoke her mind, even in her first year in Congress.

_____ Because she felt humiliated, she became a problem in the classroom.

_____ Returning to New York City was both positive and negative.

_____ Chisholm served in the House of Representatives for fifteen years.

_____ Some people thought that a woman's place was in the home and that African-Americans should stay out of politics.

_____ Chisholm won the election in a landslide victory because she had worked hard for her district.

Where did you find the sentence?

Beginning with Sentence 1, identify the paragraph and line.

Sentence	Paragraph	Line	Sentence	Paragraph	Line
_____	_____	_____	_____	_____	_____
_____	_____	_____	_____	_____	_____
_____	_____	_____	_____	_____	_____
_____	_____	_____			

List three adjectives that describe Shirley Chisholm.

1. _____

2. _____

3. _____

Share your adjectives with the members of your group.

Now work as a group to analyze the following:

What did Chisholm do?	Paragraph	What does this tell us about Chisholm?
_____	_____	_____
_____	_____	_____
_____	_____	_____
_____	_____	_____
_____		_____

What did other people say about Chisholm?
_____
_____

Look at your adjectives at the top of the page. Can you support them with sentences from the reading. What paragraph? What line?

	Adjective	Paragraph	Line
1.	_____	_____	_____
2.	_____	_____	_____
3.	_____	_____	_____

INTERPRETATION

False Statements

The following statements about the reading are incorrect. **Find** the words that make the statements incorrect and cross them out. **Replace** the incorrect words with words from the reading.

Share your responses with the members of your group. Then, **identify** the paragraph where you found the information.

___ 1. Shirley returned to Barbados to live with her parents.

___ 2. In 1963, Chisholm decided to run for the U.S. Congress.

___ 3. Shirley was moved down to the third grade because she couldn't read.

___ 4. Chisholm was a member of the U.S. Congress for ten years.

___ 5. Shirley Chisholm was the first African-American elected to the U.S. Congress.

___ 6. Chisholm learned to become a fighter in Barbados.

___ 7. Chisholm was a professor before she went into politics.

___ 8. Chisholm's parents were born in Brooklyn, New York.

CAUSES AND EFFECTS

Below are a list of causes and a list of effects from the reading. Match the two.

a. Chisholm worked hard in her political district.

b. Chisholm's parents both needed to work.

c. Chisholm was outspoken.

d. Shirley was moved down to the third grade.

e. There were many chores on the farm for the girls to do.

___ She became known as a troublemaker.

___ Shirley learned how to work hard at a young age.

___ She won the election to the state Assembly in 1963.

___ The sisters were sent to Barbados to live with their grandmother.

___ She became a problem in the classroom.

87

Listen and Scan

Listen to these paragraphs from the reading. **Scan** the paragraphs while you listen. Then, **identify** the main idea, paragraph number, and line.

Main Idea

_____

_____

Paragraph _____   Line _____

Main Idea

_____

_____

Paragraph _____   Line _____

Main Idea

_____

_____

Paragraph _____   Line _____

Notice the position of the main ideas in these paragraphs. Where are the main ideas?

Now that you have identified the main ideas, **find** the details that support them. **Write** the paragraph numbers in the column on the left. Then, **list** the details that support the main idea in each paragraph.

Paragraph   **Supporting Details**

_____   _____

Paragraph   **Supporting Details**

_____   _____

Paragraph   **Supporting Details**

_____   _____

Some of the vocabulary in the reading may be new to you. Find **synonyms** (words that have similar meanings) for the nouns below in the numbered paragraphs.
Underline the word in the reading. Then, **identify** the noun ending. Work with your classmates to find a synonym for each word.

	Word	Paragraph	Noun Ending	Synonym
1.	opponent	1	_____	_____
2.	advantages	3	_____	_____
3.	racism	4	_____	_____
4.	adjustment	6	_____	_____
5.	attention	6	_____	_____

OPPOSITES

In the numbered paragraphs, **find** the words that are the **antonyns** (or opposites) of the words listed below.

1.	Paragraph	1	overpaid	_____
2.	Paragraph	1	lazy	_____
3.	Paragraph	4	loving	_____
4.	Paragraph	4	proud	_____
5.	Paragraph	5	failed	_____
6.	Paragraph	6	encourage	_____
7.	Paragraph	7	silent	_____
8.	Paragraph	7	maximum	_____

Which words on this list are **nouns**? How do you know?

Which words are **verbs**? (Words that describe what Chisholm did.)

Which words are **adjectives**? (Words that describe a person.)

Shirley Chisholm fought for the things that she believed in. She worked hard for equal opportunities in jobs and education, especially for women.
List below some of the things that Chisholm fought for.

What are **you** willing to fight for? List some of the things that you believe in.

In Chisholm's Life

In My Life

_____   _____

_____   _____

_____   _____

Discussion Questions/ Reading Journal Topics

1. What kind of person is Chisholm? How would you describe her?

2. What do you have in common with Shirley Chisholm?

3. Does Shirley remind you of anyone you know in your family or community?

4. Is there anything you would like to ask Shirley Chisholm?

FRANK FAT

"An American Success Story"

PREREADING

What kinds of success do you admire?

Circle any areas that apply to you.

Successful Families	**Success In Work**	**Success In Sports**	**Social Success**

Look at the picture above. What kinds of success do you think this man had in his life? Can you guess his profession?

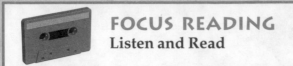
FRANK FAT: "AN AMERICAN SUCCESS STORY"

1 The story of Frank Fat's success is the story of hundreds of immigrants who came to "Gold Mountain," the state of California, to find their fortunes. But Fat did not just make his fortune for himself and his family. He also made a difference in politics in Sacramento, the capital of one of the largest states in the nation.

2 What made Fat successful? Was he a lawyer, a senator, or an assemblyman? Actually, Frank Fat was a restaurant owner who worked for 55 years to create a personal dining room for the most powerful politicians in the state! Hard work, good food, and a "megawatt smile" made Frank Fat a mover and shaker in California.

3 Dong Gai Fat first came to the West Coast from China in 1920. He was sixteen years old, and his only relative in Sacramento was the "paper father" in his pocket (the false immigration papers that said his father was a U.S. citizen). He had no family, no money, and no job. It was not a very promising beginning.

4 What did Fat have to prepare him for the future? He had determination. For three years, he worked at odd jobs in Sacramento and in the Midwest. He tried dishwashing. He picked fruit. He earned $3.00 a week doing small chores in a beauty parlor. For a while, he lived under the boardwalk near the Southern Pacific train station. After returning to China to marry, Frank came back to Sacramento to work as a waiter and restaurant manager. He didn't seem to be making much progress.

5 However, Frank Fat was learning from every experience. In the restaurants, he learned about food–how to prepare it and what people liked. He used this knowledge to open a restaurant at 806 "L" Street. All of his friends told him that it was a bad buy. "Not a good location," some said. "No one would go there," said others.

6   Frank Fat persisted. He had learned from his experience working in restaurants. He said that people wanted good food and a nice place to eat it. It was a simple recipe that worked for 55 years. Banana cream pie and New York steak became his trademarks, along with dozens of other Chinese and American dishes. As one longtime customer said, "What was so wonderful about him (was). . . he would fix whatever people wanted." Fat knew how to make people feel at home.

7   And people did feel comfortable. Just two blocks from the captitol, Frank Fat's restaurant became the gathering place for some of the most powerful legislators in California. His restaurant wasn't just a place to eat and talk. It became *the* place to "cut deals," hammer out legislation, and outline bills that would be introduced the next day in the senate. Some important pieces of legislation were first outlined on napkins in Frank Fat's restaurant! Liberal Democrats and conservative Republicans found common ground at Fat's.

8   However, Frank did much more for Sacramento than provide a meeting place for politicians. He opened additional restaurants, first in Sacramento and then in Lake Tahoe and San Diego. He was active in the community, working on projects to improve understanding between cultural groups. This interest inspired the Pacific Rim Street Festival, which is now an annual event in Sacramento. When Fat died at the age

of 92, Mayor Joe Serna said, "He was an institution in this town, and more than that, just a great, great man."

9   What made Frank Fat successful? Like most immigrants, Fat was hardworking and persistent. He didn't give up, even in hard times. But Fat also had a philosophy which created positive energy in his workplace and in the city. "Treat people right," he often said. "Good things will come back to you." And they did.

LISTEN AND SCAN

Listen to the questions on the tape. Stop the tape after each question. Scan for information, and write your answers on the lines below.

1. How old was Frank when he came to California?

2. What jobs did he find when he came to California?

3. Where was his famous restaurant?

4. What did the mayor say when Frank Fat died?

	Paragraph	Line	Response
1.	_____	____	_____ _____
2.	_____	____	_____ _____
3.	_____	____	_____ _____
4.	_____	____	_____ _____

The sentences below are **paraphrases.** A paraphrase is a sentence with the same meaning as another sentence, but using different words.

Work with your partner to find the sentences in the reading with the same meaning.
Underline those sentences.
Then, number the paraphrases from 1 to 10, in the order in which they occur in the reading.

_____ Frank Fat arrived in California from Asia in 1920.

_____ Fat was a dedicated community activist who tried to improve intercultural relations.

_____ Fat stated that people enjoyed eating well in a pleasant environment.

_____ Fat did part-time work for several years on the West Coast and in the Midwest.

_____ Legislators wrote bills at Frank Fat's.

_____ Friends and acquaintances said that the restaurant would not be successful.

_____ Fat's career wasn't moving forward.

_____ Both liberals and conservatives were able to discuss issues at Frank Fat's restaurant.

_____ At sixteen, Fat had no family in Sacramento when he arrived.

_____ Frank Fat, like other immigrants, worked hard and didn't give up.

Where did you find the sentence?
Beginning with Sentence 1, identify the paragraph and line.

Sentence	Paragraph	Line	Sentence	Paragraph	Line
____	____	____	____	____	____
____	____	____	____	____	____
____	____	____	____	____	____
____	____	____	____	____	____
____	____	____	____	____	____

List three adjectives that describe Frank Fat.

1. _____

2. _____

3. _____

Share your adjectives with the members of your group.

Now work as a group to analyze the following:

What did Fat do?	Paragraph	What does this tell us about Fat?
_____	_____	_____
_____	_____	_____
_____	_____	_____

What did Fat say?

_____

_____

What did other people say about Fat?

_____

_____

Look at your adjectives at the top of the page. Can you support them with sentences from the reading? What paragraph? What line?

	Adjective	Paragraph	Line
1.	_____	____	____
2.	_____	____	____
3.	_____	____	____

INTERPRETATION

False Statements

The following statements about the reading are **incorrect**. **Find** the words that make the statements incorrect and cross them out. **Replace** the incorrect words with the appropriate words from the reading.

Share your responses with the members of your group. Then, **identify** the paragraph where you found the information. **Write** the number of the paragraph on the line before each statement.

___ 1. When he arrived in California, Frank Fat carried his birth certificate in his pocket.

___ 2. Frank Fat's restaurant provided a place for Democrats to meet.

___ 3. Frank's friends approved of the location of his first restaurant.

___ 4. Fat lived with his sister near the train station.

___ 5. Frank Fat was a successful state senator.

___ 6. Frank returned to China to look for a better job.

___ 7. Fat served only Chinese dishes in his restaurant.

___ 8. Fat did not believe in community activism.

CAUSES AND EFFECTS

Below are a list of causes and a list of effects from the reading. Match the two.

a. Fat fixed whatever people wanted in his restaurant.

b. Frank worked as a dishwasher, waiter, and manager.

c. Fat was very active in the Sacramento community.

d. Fat had false immigration papers.

e. Frank wanted to improve understanding between cultural groups.

___ Fat became "an institution."

___ Fat was able to come to the United States.

___ The Pacific Rim Street Festival began.

___ Frank learned about food.

___ People were comfortable in his restaurant.

Listen and Scan
Listen to these paragraphs from the reading. **Scan** the paragraphs while you listen. Then, **identify** the main idea, paragraph number, and line.

Main Idea

_____

_____

Paragraph _____   Line ___

Main Idea

_____

_____

Paragraph _____   Line ___

Main Idea

_____

_____

Paragraph _____   Line ___

Notice the position of the main ideas in these paragraphs. Is the main idea always in the same place in each paragraph?

Now that you have identified the main ideas, **find** the details that support them.

Write the paragraph numbers in the column on the left. Then, **list** the details that support the main idea in each paragraph.

Paragraph	Supporting Details
_____	_____
Paragraph	**Supporting Details**
_____	_____
Paragraph	**Supporting Details**
_____	_____

WORD WATCH

Some of the vocabulary in the reading may be new to you. Find **synonyms** (words that have similar meanings) for the nouns below in the numbered paragraphs. **Underline** the word in the reading. Then, **identify** the noun ending. Work with your classmates to find a synonym for each word.

Word	Paragraph	Noun Ending	Synonym
1. politicians	2	_____	_____
2. determination	4	_____	_____
3. knowledge	5	_____	_____
4. trademarks	6	_____	_____
5. legislation	7	_____	_____

MATCHING

Match the adjectives on the left with the **nouns** that they describe on the right. **Find** the paragraphs in which these words occur.

Then, **write** the paragraph numbers below.

Paragraph   Noun

_____ _____	1. conservative a. recipe
_____ _____	2. persistent b. beginning
_____ _____	3. powerful c. dining room
_____ _____	4. simple d. Republicans
_____ _____	5. promising e. Frank Fat
_____ _____	6. personal f. legislators

Positives and Negatives

Make a list of words from the reading that describe Frank Fat. **Identify** these words as positive**(+)** or negative**(-)** by circling the appropriate symbol.

_____ + - _____ + -

_____ + - _____ + -

Frank Fat believed in the value of hard work and a positive attitude. He believed that "treating people right" would make the difference between success and failure. Do you agree with Fat?

What other qualities are necessary for success?
List a few of those qualities below.

_____

_____

_____

_____

_____

_____

_____

Discussion Questions/ Reading Journal Topics

1. Do you think Frank Fat was lucky?

2. When people are successful, is it because of luck or hard work?

3. Why is it important to treat people right?

4. Why is this chapter called "An American Success Story"? Do you agree?

5. Who does Frank Fat remind you of in your community?

BILL COSBY

"If you stand still, you disappear."

PREREADING

What do you think Bill Cosby was talking about when he made the statement above? Do you ever feel that you are "standing still"? What are some areas of your life in which you want to make progress or "move forward"?
Circle any areas that apply to you.

In My Social Life	**In Art Skills**	**In English In Music**	**In Math**

Look at the picture of this actor/educator. Cosby is not just an actor or entertainer. He has been successful in many different careers–and unsuccessful in others!
List three careers in which you might be successful.

1. _____
2. _____
3. _____

BILL COSBY: "IF YOU STAND STILL, YOU DISAPPEAR."

1 Bill Cosby's life has been a series of successes and remarkable "firsts." Just four years after his debut as a stand-up comedian in a small Philadelphia cafe, he earned a lead role in "I Spy," becoming the first African-American to star in a dramatic series on television. From then on, his progress never stopped. He zoomed from one exciting opportunity to another: acting, writing, producing, and making Americans laugh.

2 However, success did not come quickly or easily to Cosby. In fact, before he began to find his way, he had a lot of failures. In school, he was known as a smart kid who was more interested in getting laughs than in getting good grades. He dropped out of high school in his junior year after failing many classes. He lost several jobs because he couldn't seem to take the work seriously. It wasn't until Bill joined the Navy that he began to find himself. He realized that he needed to grow in some new directions.

3 Bill Cosby, the first of four sons born to Anna and William Cosby, Sr., was born in 1937. He grew up in a poor neighborhood in Philadelphia where hard work was expected and necessary. When Bill Cosby was still in elementary school, his father left home to join the Navy because he couldn't find a steady job. His mother worked twelve hours a day as a maid to provide food and clothing for her children. Bill helped out by working at odd jobs after school and on weekends and taking care of his brothers at home. Bill may have slacked off in school, but at home he pulled his own weight.

4   During his high school years, when Bill seemed determined to fail, he was working hard at home. His ability to work hard paid off years later when he decided to go to college. At Temple University, Cosby was an outstanding athlete, competing on basketball, football, and track teams. But most importantly, he was succeeding academically. His mother breathed a sigh of relief!

5   Imagine Mrs. Cosby's dismay when Bill announced, in his junior year, that he was dropping out of college to try a career as a comedian! To his mother, it seemed that Bill was throwing his opportunities out of the window. But Bill wasn't just getting laughs to pass the time, as he did in high school. He was working hard at his new career, and within three years, he was a familiar face on television.

6   At the same time, he continued working on comedy routines, based on his experiences growing up. His albums, "I Started Out as a Child," "Revenge," "Fat Albert," and over a dozen other titles, grew out of family and street memories from Philadelphia days. His story-telling techniques, learned from his mother and grandfather, and his own wacky sense of humor captivated audiences all over the country. Bill Cosby was on his way to becoming a household word.

7   As usual, however, Cosby wasn't happy just doing the "same old same old."He decided to branch out in new directions. "I Spy" was just the first of many television series in which Bill Cosby starred. The most famous, featuring the likeable Huxtable family, was "The Cosby Show."

8 During the same years, Bill took lead roles in a variety of movies: "Uptown Saturday Night," "A Piece of the Action," and "Ghost Dad," to name only a few. And when he wasn't acting and telling jokes, he was taking care of some unfinished business from his youth: Bill went back to college, earning his BA, his Master's degree and, finally, his doctorate in education in 1976. Bill didn't know how to stand still!

9 Some people are slow starters, but once they get going, they can't stop. Bill Cosby is one of these people. He is a successful comedian, actor, writer, speaker, and producer. He is also a dedicated father and husband. He has managed to achieve great things in several different areas, and he hasn't disappeared yet!

LISTEN AND SCAN

Listen to the questions on the tape. Stop the tape after each question. Scan for information, and write your answers on the lines below.

1. What did Bill's mother do to earn a living when he was growing up?

2. When did Bill finally begin to "find himself"?

3. Where did Bill Cosby begin attending college?

4. Where did Bill learn his story-telling techniques?

Paragraph	Line	Response
1. _____	____	_____ _____
2. _____	____	_____ _____
3. _____	____	_____ _____
4. _____	____	_____ _____

PUTTING THINGS IN ORDER

The sentences below describe events in the life of Bill Cosby. They are paraphrases of sentences in the reading.

Work with your partner to find the events in the reading. Underline those sentences. Then, number the sentences from 1 to 10, in chronological order.

_____ Bill left college to try a career as a comedian.

_____ Cosby became the first African-American actor to play a leading role in a dramatic television series.

_____ Bill enlisted in the Navy.

_____ Because Bill's father couldn't find work, he joined the Navy.

_____ "The Cosby Show" became Cosby's most successful television series.

_____ Bill helped his mother by taking care of his brothers and working at part-time jobs in the evenings and on weekends.

_____ William Cosby, Jr. received his doctorate in education.

_____ Discouraged by his failing grades, Bill didn't finish high school.

_____ Cosby excelled in basketball, football, and track.

_____ Bill enjoyed getting laughs but didn't take himself seriously.

Where did you find the sentence?

Beginning with Sentence 1, identify the paragraph and line.

Sentence	Paragraph	Line	Sentence	Paragraph	Line
_____	_____	_____	_____	_____	_____
_____	_____	_____	_____	_____	_____
_____	_____	_____	_____	_____	_____
_____	_____	_____	_____	_____	_____
_____	_____	_____	_____	_____	_____

List three adjectives that describe Bill Cosby.

1. _____

2. _____

3. _____

Share your adjectives with the members of your group.

Now work as a group to analyze the following:

What did Cosby do?	Paragraph	What does this tell us about him?
_____	_____	_____
_____	_____	_____
_____	_____	_____
_____	_____	_____
_____	_____	_____

What did other people think about Bill?

_____

_____

Look at your adjectives at the top of the page. Can you support them with sentences from the reading? What paragraph? What line?

	Adjective	Paragraph	Line
1.	_____	_____	_____
2.	_____	_____	_____
3.	_____	_____	_____

False Statements

The following statements about the reading are **incorrect**. **Find** the words that make the statements incorrect and cross them out. **Replace** the incorrect words with the appropriate words from the reading.

Share your responses with the members of your group. Then, **identify** the paragraph where you found the information. **Write** the number of the paragraph on the line before each statement.

___ 1. Cosby graduated with his BA from Temple University.

___ 2. Cosby's first television series was "The Cosby Show."

___ 3. In school, Bill was known as a smart kid who took schoolwork seriously.

___ 4. Bill returned to college in 1976.

___ 5. Cosby's comedy albums were based on his experiences in college.

___ 6. Bill began to find himself and his life direction in high school.

___ 7. Cosby grew up in a comfortable, middle-class neighborhood.

___ 8. When he was growing up, Bill slacked off at school and at home.

CAUSES AND EFFECTS

Below are a list of causes and a list of effects from the reading. Match the two.

a. Bill learned story-telling techniques from his mother and her father.

b. William Cosby, Sr. couldn't find steady work.

c. Bill's mother worked twelve-hour days as a maid.

d. Bill Cosby, Jr. joined the Navy.

e. Bill Cosby doesn't stand still.

___ Bill hasn't disappeared yet!

___ He found new directions for his life.

___ Cosby captivated audiences all over the country.

___ Cosby's father joined the Navy.

___ Bill took care of his brothers at home.

Listen and Scan
Listen to these paragraphs from the reading. **Scan** the paragraphs while you listen. Then, **identify** the main idea, paragraph number, and line.

Main Idea

_____

_____

Paragraph _____   Line ___

Main Idea

_____

_____

Paragraph _____   Line ___

Main Idea

_____

_____

Paragraph _____   Line ___

Notice the position of the main ideas in these paragraphs. Is the main idea always in the same place in each paragraph?

Now that you have identified the main ideas, **find** the details that support them. **Write** the paragraph numbers in the column on the left. Then, **list** the details that support the main idea in each paragraph.

Paragraph   **Supporting Details**

_____   _____

Paragraph   **Supporting Details**

_____   _____

Paragraph   **Supporting Details**

_____   _____

Some of the vocabulary in the reading may be new to you.
In the groups of words below, **circle** the **one** word that does not fit in the group.
Share your results with your partner.

In and Out

1. remarkable	outstanding	poor
2. pulled his own weight	slacked off	dropped out
3. successes	failures	firsts
4. doctorate	comedy	BA
5. getting laughs	working hard	getting his BA
6. determined	famous	household word

With your class or in groups, **identify** the **part of speech** of each group of words and **discuss** why some words do not fit in.

OPPOSITES

In the numbered paragraphs, find the words that are the **opposites** of the words listed below.

1.	Paragraph	4	failing	_____
2.	Paragraph	1	boring	_____
3.	Paragraph	4	poor	_____
4.	Paragraph	5	pleasure	_____
5.	Paragraph	9	move ahead	_____
6.	Paragraph	3	unneeded	_____
7.	Paragraph	5	unknown	_____
8.	Paragraph	7	unpleasant	_____

Positives and Negatives

Make a list of words from the reading that describe Bill Cosby. **Identify** these words as positive(+) or negative(-) by circling the appropriate symbol.

_____	+	-	_____	+ -
_____	+	-	_____	+ -
_____	+	-	_____	+ -

As Bill Cosby says, he doesn't believe in "standing still." He believes that people should try new things, even if they are already successful.

What new things did Cosby try after his first success?

List a few of those things below.

What new things would you like to try at some point in your life?

List a few of them below.

Cosby's New Tries

_____

_____

_____

_____

_____

_____

My New Tries

_____

_____

_____

_____

_____

_____

Discussion Questions/ Reading Journal Topics

1. Do you know anyone like Cosby, who has started out with failure and then been successful?

2. Do you known anyone like Cosby, who has been successful in several different careers?

3. What characteristics made Cosby successful?

4. In what ways are you similar to Bill Cosby?

SHIRLEY CHISHOLM, FRANK FAT, AND BILL COSBY

Three Lives: Chisholm, Fat, and Cosby

PREREADING

All of these people had dreams of success. Even when other people didn't understand, they continued to follow their dreams.

What do **you** have in common with these people?
Circle any nouns that apply to you.

Persistence   Belief In Themselves   Hardworking Parents

            Courage   Community Connections

Look at the pictures above. What adjectives describe all three people?
List your adjectives below.

1. _____

2. _____

3. _____

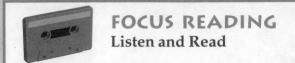

THREE LIVES: CHISHOLM, FAT, AND COSBY

Fitting In Information
In which paragraphs do the following sentences belong?

FOCUS READING ONE

Listen and **read** the follow sentences with details about Chisholm. Be ready to **share** your information about your focus person with your group.

Fighting Shirley Chisholm: Unbought and Unbossed

1. She also learned the power of political organization at the meetings of the Universal Negro Improvement Association, which she attended with her father.

    Paragraph ____

2. Shirley learned to make the best spitballs in school.

    Paragraph ____

3. During her four years in the State Assembly, Chisholm proposed nine bills, four of which were signed into law.

    Paragraph ____

4. Years later, she was the first member of her family to attend college.

    Paragraph ____

5. Her father was a baker's helper, and her mother worked as a seamstress and a cleaning woman.

    Paragraph ____

6. With the help of a tutor, she caught up with the rest of the sixth grade class.

    Paragraph ____

7. One of her successes at Brooklyn College was the debating prize, which was presented to Shirley by Eleanor Roosevelt, ambassador to the United Nations at the time.

    Paragraph ____

8. She was the first African-American woman to serve in the U.S. Congress.

    Paragraph ____

In which paragraphs do the following sentences belong?

FOCUS READING TWO

Listen and **read** the following sentences with details about Frank Fat. Be ready to **share** your information about your focus person with your group.

Frank Fat: An American Success Story

1. Some people regard Frank Fat as the father of the restaurant industry in Sacramento.

    Paragraph _____

2. In 1939, this was a slum area in Sacramento.

    Paragraph _____

3. Sacramento has lost not just a successful business owner, but also a friend.

    Paragraph _____

4. In his restaurant, California lawmakers could play cards and exchange ideas.

    Paragraph _____

5. In another community effort, the Frank Fat Endowment Fund was set up to fund research on kidney disease.

    Paragraph _____

6. Twelve different governors have enjoyed good food and good company at Frank Fat's.

    Paragraph _____

7. He saw it advertized for sale, borrowed the money, and bought the restaurant for $2,000.

    Paragraph _____

8. China Camp and Fat City were two other successful Sacramento restaurants.

    Paragraph _____

In which paragraphs do the following sentences belong?

FOCUS READING THREE

Listen and **read** the following sentences with details about Cosby. Be ready to **share** your information about your focus person with your group.

Bill Cosby: "If You Stand Still, You Disappear."

1. In the Navy, Bill studied and finally earned his high school diploma.

   Paragraph _____

2. He earned a four-year athletic scholarship.

   Paragraph _____

3. Cosby's friends from boyhood–Fat Albert and Wierd Harold–returned to life in his comedy routines.

   Paragraph _____

4. Cosby was performing at "The Cellar," a room in the Underground, where he worked as a bartender.

   Paragraph _____

5. In this series, Bill played a super-smart spy who spoke several languages.

   Paragraph _____

6. He has written several books about important life stages, including *Fatherhood* and *Time Flies*, a book about getting older.

   Paragraph _____

7. This show won many Emmy Awards for "Outstanding Comedy Series."

   Paragraph _____

8. "Teaching kids and providing a good example for them is very important to me," says Cosby.

   Paragraph _____

Sharing Information

Each person in your group has read and listened to information about **one** of the focus people. Take turns sharing your information. In your own words, tell your group members the new information you have learned.

The sentences on pages 112–114 of this chapter give details about three lives: Chisholm, Fat, and Cosby. These details are **not** in chronological order. Where do these details fit in the readings on these three people?

Work with your group members to find the paragraphs where these details fit in the readings in Chapters 9, 10, and 11. Then write the **paragraph number** next to each of the detail sentences. Now enter this information on the grid below.

	CHISHOLM Paragraph	FAT Paragraph	COSBY Paragraph
Sentence 1			
Sentence 2			
Sentence 3			
Sentence 4			
Sentence 5			
Sentence 6			
Sentence 7			
Sentence 8			

Look back at the three adjectives you listed at the beginning of the chapter. Can you support these adjectives? Fill in the grid below, using information from chapters 9, 10, and 11.

1   Adjective: _____   **What did he/she say or do?**

   Chisholm   _____

   Fat   _____

   Cosby   _____

2   Adjective: _____   **What did he/she say or do?**

   Chisholm   _____

   Fat   _____

   Cosby   _____

3   Adjective: _____   **What did he/she say or do?**

   Chisholm   _____

   Fat   _____

   Cosby   _____

Share and compare your information with the members of your group.

Can You Prove It?

The following statements are **similarities**. Some of the statements you can prove (or support) from the readings in chapters 9, 10, and 11. Other statements cannot be proven from the readings.

If you think that the readings support the statement, write **yes**. Then give the page and paragraph numbers to support the statement. If you can't prove the statement, write **no**.

Page	Paragraph	Yes/No	Statement
_____	_____	_____	1. Both Cosby and Fat had to work as teenagers.
_____	_____	_____	2. The parents of both Chisholm and Fat were immigrants.
_____	_____	_____	3. Both Bill Cosby and Frank Fat were businessmen.
_____	_____	_____	4. The mothers of both Chisholm and Cosby worked outside the home to help support the family.
_____	_____	_____	5. Shirley Chisholm and Frank Fat were both active in their communities.
_____	_____	_____	6. Chisholm and Cosby were smart, but they both had some problems in school.
_____	_____	_____	7. Fat and Cosby both grew up in large families.
_____	_____	_____	8. Shirley Chisholm and Frank Fat both worked closely with legislators during their careers.

**Share your responses with the members of your group.
Do all of you agree?**

MEMORY CHECK

Listen to the following statements. Stop the tape after each sentence. Who is the statement about–Shirley Chisholm, Frank Fat, or Bill Cosby ? Mark an **X** in the appropriate box on the chart. Listen more than once if necessary. Use your book to help you.

Sentence	Chisholm	Fat	Cosby
1			
2			
3			
4			
5			
6			
7			

Below are some of the adjectives from chapters 9, 10, and 11. Work with a partner to find each adjective. Identify the adjectives by chapter and paragraph number. Then use the adjective in a new sentence of your own.

Adjective	Chapter	Paragraph	New Sentence
1. dedicated	_____	_____	_____
			_____
2. persistent	_____	_____	_____
			_____
3. outspoken	_____	_____	_____
			_____
4. "megawatt"	_____	_____	_____
			_____
5. outstanding	_____	_____	_____
			_____
6. ashamed	_____	_____	_____
			_____

Suffixes

There are many posssible endings for **adjectives** (words that describe) in English. One common ending is **-ful**. Another is **-able**. Working with your group members, take one of the three chapters each and see how many adjectives with **one** of these endings you can find. Then, find the adjectives below. **Identify** the adjectives by page number and paragraph number.

Word	Page	Paragraph
likeable	_____	_____
hateful	_____	_____
remarkable	_____	_____
powerful	_____	_____

Shirley Chisholm was an influential legislator, at both the state and national levels. Frank Fat developed a very successful restaurant business, providing a place for California legislators to meet. Bill Cosby became one of the nation's highest paid entertainers and went on to accomplish major achievements in film and education. All three people have tried to give something back to their communities.

When you are successful in later life, what would you like to do for your community?

List a few things that you would like to do for your community.

_____

_____

_____

_____

_____

_____

_____

_____

Discussion Questions/ Reading Journal Topics

1. Why do you think these three leaders were so successful? Choose one or two words to describe all three.

2. What similarities do they share?

3. Which person do **you** identify with? Why?

4. In what ways are **you** similar to one or all of these people?